Sunday Is for the Sun,
Monday Is for the Moon

SUNDAY IS FOR THE SUN, MONDAY IS FOR THE MOON

Teaching Reading, One Teacher & Thirty Children at a Time

By Sandra Priest Rose and Glen Nelson

Literacy is not a handy knack. It is a moral condition. The ability to read attentively, reflectively, and judiciously is equally the ability to be attentive, reflective, and judicious. For the sake of just and sane living, literacy is not an optional adornment. It is a necessity. It is the wholesome nourishment of the mind, by which it may grow strong enough to be master of the will and not its slave, the judge of desire and not its procurer, the censor of sentiment and not its tool, and the inquisitor of belief, and not its flack. It is our only path to whatever wisdom we can have, which is our only path to whatever goodness we can know, which is our only path to whatever happiness we can enjoy.

R. MITCHELL *Underground Grammarian, 1987*

Table of Contents

Saving American Education:

TEACHING READING, ONE TEACHER AND THIRTY CHILDREN AT A TIME

THIS IS THE STORY OF HOW ONE ORGANIZATION STROVE TO quietly revolutionize the teaching of reading in New York City. This book describes a program that can be easily duplicated all over the United States.

It requires a willingness on the part of the mentor to be trained in a new approach to teaching and to do a great deal of hard work.

It requires equal willingness on the part of the classroom teachers to undergo this rigorous, supportive training in their classrooms. As the classroom teachers quickly see the advances their students make, their initial skepticism turns to enthusiasm.

The program requires principals who are willing to try something they know has been missing from their instructional program. Administrators and school boards also know that if students learn to read, write, spell and comprehend well in kindergarten through third grade, they are on their way to a successful life at every stage.

All of this requires relatively few dollars. Pencils, paper, chalk and books are the necessary ingredients—lots of each—because writing becomes fun, and the power of unlocking words and meanings draws students into reading many books of increasing difficulty.

The research of Linda Darling-Hammond (see Appendix) at Stanford University has shown that a large percentage of classroom teachers receive as little as two days of training per year on the content of the subjects they teach. The report states that "Effective professional development is intensive, ongoing and connected to practice," and "focuses on the teaching and learning of specific academic content..." This is precisely the nature of the Reading Reform Foundation mission.

The Reading Reform Foundation program, consisting of 160 hours of training that classroom teachers receive, is a model that should be replicated throughout the United States.

The children benefit hugely, as can be seen from the test scores appended to the end of this book. The classroom teacher benefits from a training that is useful for the rest of his or her professional life.

Thirty years of Reading Reform Foundation's experience in teaching approximately 2,000 children per year and training thousands of teachers in courses, workshops and conferences has shown irrefutably that children of all social and economic backgrounds can learn and excel.

Reading Reform Foundation has shown the way. It CAN be done and MUST be done. As a nation, we cannot fail our children any longer.

Practicing the sounds of written English

CHAPTER I

A Lively Classroom –

THE READING REFORM FOUNDATION WAY

TWENTY-ONE STUDENTS FILE INTO A KINDERGARTEN CLASSROOM at Community School 134 in the Bronx in New York City. They walk two by two. They take off their coats and stow them away in cubbies built into a large walk-in closet. They are dressed identically, or nearly so, in uniforms of light blue shirts and dark blue pants and skirts. A few of the students wear clothing that approximates the school uniform, substituted with a t-shirt and blue jeans. All the students find their seats quickly at three rows of small, separated tables that face the chalkboard. Behind each, two students sit facing front with an additional student or two sitting at each end. There is a sheet of paper in front of each student as well as a sharpened pencil. They prepare to get started. This all happens silently and quickly. Within thirty seconds the students, who had been outside at recess playing minutes earlier, have settled down to work.

The classroom itself is large and filled with sunlight on a chilly winter day. An entire wall of windows on the south side of the room floods the space with brightness. The walls are papered with pictures and samples of writing that are displayed on every available vertical surface. The ceiling is high, perhaps twenty feet above the students.

The blackboard that stretches the width of the room is so completely covered in learning materials that its slate surface is entirely hidden. Posters display coins and currency, a large face of a clock with moveable hands, and illustrations from books. Letters of the alphabet and numbers scroll across the top of the board. There are a few chairs for adult visitors that look surprisingly large relative to the Lilliputian scale of the rest of the room. This is kindergarten.

A lovely woman, perhaps in her early thirties, steps confidently in front of the classroom. She is Mrs. Karen Cintron, and she launches into the lesson like a racehorse out of the starting gate. First is the alphabet, which they chant, alternating two letters at a time, between teacher and students, "A, B." "C, D." "E, F," and so on, until they reach the end. It is breathlessly fast and loud. The students hear Mrs. Cintron say, "Good," and they move instantly to the next task, a listing of all the vowels and the possible sounds that each makes. The students practically shout the responses in a choral unison. "Good," says Mrs. Cintron.

Oral blending is next. The teacher says two sounds, "f," "a," and the students blend these sounds together. She says ten combinations of sounds and says, "Good." She points to the list of sight words, which students say in unison. For the last few words she asks the students for sentences with those words. She points to the suffix chart and the children call out, "suffix -s means more than one, suffix –ing means happening now."

The teacher picks up a thick stack of index cards and holds them at chest level, and she rotates the cards one by one to the end of the stack. Each card has a picture and a letter or a combination of letters, which the students sound out, again, at breakneck speed. The cards, three dozen or so, pass by quickly. At each, the students say the picture name and the sound on the card. The first cards are straightforward: the letter *r* invokes the class, "Rrrrr." The letter *b* triggers an explosive sound, "Buh." But the sounds become increasingly more complex. The class distinguishes clearly between the sounds of *ch* and *sh*, for example, and also when *ai* and *ay* are used (rain/ai, tray/ay).

When Mrs. Cintron gets to the card, *ay*, the students say "*tray/ay*". And so it goes as she propels her way through the pile of picture cards, then letter cards. As they proceed, Mrs. Cintron repeats some of the sounds that aren't perfected yet by the group, and the students hone in on exact pronunciation. Everyone in the class is participating. The entire stack of cards is dispatched in minutes.

Now Mrs. Cintron is at the front of the room and begins to write the word *clap* for visual blending. The teacher writes on a dotted-line wipe-off board. As she writes, the students sound out each letter deliberately and carefully. She asks a student, Jonathan, to sound it out. "*c*," "*llll*", "*a*," "*pppp*," then, "*cl*", "*claaa*", and finally, "*claaaap*," "*clap!*" As he reads the word, some of the students have a surprised look on their faces—not all of the students; just a few—as if a little light has gone on in their heads, an "Oh, I get it."

Mrs. Sandra Gittens, a Reading Reform Foundation consultant, takes over part of the lesson and announces that the class will be learning a new way to spell the sound *c* as in *ck*. She teaches them how to write the letters *ck*. They repeat the sound exactly, and over the next few minutes, they practice reading the sound as it occurs in different words. On the board, with solid and broken lines across it, she writes the letter *c*, then the letter *k*.

They raise their arms in the air, as if they are holding an imaginary pencil. Together they draw the letters in space very slowly. First the *c*, with an even curve. "Again," the teacher says, "Again." They move on to the *k*. The students' little arms are stretched as high as they will go to begin. In the air they draw a long, vertical line and then the teacher instructs them precisely where to connect the slanted lines of the *k*. "Again. Again." Then they are asked to pick up their pencils, and they write the letters on paper. "If you made a mistake, cross it out and try again," she says. The room is completely silent. The students are concentrating on their work.

They learn that *ck* can only be used after a single vowel, never at the beginning of a word. Mrs. Gittens writes the word *neck* on the board. She asks students to "code" it. First they break the word into sounds, "*nnn*," "*eh*," "*ck*", "*neck*." She draws a line under the *ck* and reinforces the sound that they have been learning today. As the teacher sounds out other words, *rock, back,* and *sick,* the students sound them out for reading. They also spell words with *ck* onto their paper.

Vocabulary practice begins as the teacher says a word, "drum," uses it in a sentence and calls on a student to spell each sound letter-by-letter as the class writes it. They do this quietly with a few words.

All of this happens rapidly. There is a formality to the lesson, and because of the speed of it, it feels something like a drill, but there is also compassion. When a student doesn't seem to understand a concept, a teacher kneels down by her side and helps her. When another student seems distracted and his leg starts kicking the radiator compulsively, the mentor, Mrs. Gittens, who is working alongside Mrs. Cintron, places her hand on his shoulder for a second and he rejoins the lesson. A pencil falls to the ground, a student mispronounces a word, and a boy momentarily goes quiet as his classmates are reciting, but each rejoins the spirited lesson.

Papers and pencils are collected, and each student is given a little reading book. The name of the book is *Al.* Al is an alligator. The pace of the class and the atmosphere in the room change. Some of the formality dissipates, and in its place enters curiosity. "Who wants to read?" the teacher asks, and the hands shoot up. In an instant, every child's hand is waving excitedly. Each page has a half dozen or so words on it. As a student is called upon, he reads aloud, his finger touching the words on the page as he proceeds. "Mr. Joseph," "Miss Mariah," the teacher selects students. As they read the story about an alligator that gets into quite a bit of trouble, a sort of Curious George with teeth, the class stops to analyze what is going on and what they understand. After a reader finishes a page, the teacher repeats aloud what the child has read. If a word requires extra attention, the child who is reading sounds it out. Finally, the book is finished. Every student has had at least one chance to read aloud—Jonathan, Gabriel, Rafael, Unique, Joseph, Reginald, Tynique, Steven, Jacob, Mariah, Courtney, Xavier, Hailey, Jared, Dielsa, Daisy, and the others, including one little boy whose name is Knowledge. Together they discuss the characters and the ideas that they discovered in the story. And then, as abruptly as it began, the class time is over.

Reading Reform Foundation of New York is responsible for the teaching of that small class in the Bronx; in numerous other New York City schools in Brooklyn, Queens, and Manhattan, and in the Westchester County towns of Mt. Vernon and Port Chester. Mrs. Gittens is one of the Foundation's thirty-five mentors who travel to the schools twice each week. Currently 2,000 children per year benefit from Reading Reform-trained teachers. Seventy-eight teachers are receiving training now in 23 schools. There are 300 teachers taking Reading Reform courses.

Reading Reform Foundation goes into schools and works with teachers as mentors. To date, 30,000 students have been taught with Reading Reform Foundation's methodology, and 20,000 teachers have attended Reading Reform Foundation's annual conference and taken graduate-level courses. Almost 1,200 teachers have been part of the in-school teacher-training program.

Reading Reform Foundation's teaching consultants are mentors who have been trained to guide teachers of students K through 3 in some of the most challenging neighborhoods in New York and Westchester County. The mentors thoroughly train teachers in a program of reading. The mentor-consultants sit with the classroom teachers in twice-a-week teacher preparation periods, and together they map out the specifics of each lesson that will be taught. The mentors provide reading materials for the classroom, bringing paper and even sharpened pencils for the students. The consultants monitor the children's progress, and at the end of the year Reading Reform Foundation sends a report to the principals of the schools. That is the work of the Foundation, and this volume about their efforts is a window into what they do, why they do it, and how it is accomplished. It is not an easy job, but they do it with passion.

A Bronx Neighborhood

This classroom, K-III, is part of C.S. (Community School) 134, George W. Bristow Elementary School. It is a large, four-story brick building on Bristow Street in the South Bronx. A few blocks away is the elevated subway train running on the Seventh Avenue line, and a dozen blocks to the north is the Bronx Zoo. The community's buildings are a mixture of old and new. Across the street from the school, a row of nearly-identical single family, two-story homes rest side by side, and down the block are taller brick buildings constructed early in the last century. In the neighborhood, multiple building complexes have been completed recently, built to house middle- and lower-income families. The streets are quiet in mid-day, almost deserted.

The Morrisania section of the South Bronx, where the school is located, is in the southwestern area of the borough. The school population is 44% African-American, 55% Latino, and 1% 'other'. The school population is 94.3% eligible for the Free Lunch Program. The median household income in 2009 in Morrisania was $18,329, compared to the Bronx as a whole, $32,893. The percentage of the population below the poverty level in Morrisania is 48.0%, contrasted with the Bronx as a whole, 30.7%.

In some ways the challenges of the neighborhood are not apparent inside Community School 134 itself, which is bright, well-kept, clean, spacious, and organized. In appearance, the facilities are similar to many public schools old and new in the largest city in the country.

This cleanliness and order are often unacknowledged in the press. In the classrooms the students appear to be perfectly happy and successful in their studies. All seems to be going well. If this is the case, much credit goes to its fine teachers and staff, and especially to Principal Kenneth Thomas, a veteran public school administrator who exudes a beautiful mixture of kindness and confidence.

Still, some of the facts of urban life that Principal Thomas has to manage would make many other educators quake. Within the school boundaries is the largest concentration of public assistance shelters in the city. These shelters for battered women, the homeless and their families affect the school directly as the children residing in shelters enter the C.S. 134 student body. A particular challenge is the fact that, according to city policy, residents of a shelter may only remain there for six months, and then they must move on, sometimes to other boroughs entirely, and to other shelters. The result is that the children of the shelters are constantly uprooted and continually forced to change schools, teachers and friends. To remain in the school, some have been required to travel from Brooklyn, many miles away. Principal Thomas describes the gravity of the situation when he notes that for these children, school is the one stable thing in their lives.

There is more at stake, therefore, than simply teaching a child to read. Or, said another way, teaching a child to read is more than about reading.

Classrooms look different and function differently these days. Students' desks no longer face front; they are grouped together with handfuls of students facing each other, the fronts of their desks touching each other. The teacher's desk, if there is one at all, is in the back of the room. The old blackboard is covered up with posters. It is merely another wall. Chalk has all but vanished. Instead of the blackboard, there are white boards attached to printers. There are also computer terminals, televisions and video players.

One might think that the classrooms in C.S. 134 are different because of their community demographics. One could extrapolate that this approach to reading, writing, and spelling has an undercurrent of remedial education. But those assumptions are untrue. Instead, the method of teaching these kindergarten children (as well as first through third graders, who are learning the same concepts using the same approach) is quite simply this: for the teachers and the children to discover together the regularities of English spelling and pronunciation as a precursor to reading. This is the process by which children can become experts in reading, writing, spelling and comprehension, all of which gives them advanced tools for their future.

IN 2009 RETIRED TEACHER MAUREEN DOYLE WROTE:

"Parents who see me on the street nowadays tell me *what a difference it made in spelling, reading, and writing* for their now young-adult children."

CHAPTER II

Reading History Highlights

READING EDUCATION HAS A LONG AND COLORFUL HISTORY IN the United States. Reading Reform Foundation of New York stands outside of much of the battle between one approach and another. Reading Reform Foundation's concern is that children learn and learn well. Yet, it is helpful to see the value of what can be accomplished in a classroom by briefly reviewing the history of reading education in America.

In 1647, a law was enacted in the General Court of Massachusetts that mandated the teaching of reading. Every township with 50 or more residents were to "appoint one within their towne to teach all such children as shall resort to him to write and reade, whose wages shall be paid either by parents or masters of such children, or by the inhabitants in generall..." At the time, illiteracy meant an inability to read the scriptures. Reading, then, was a tool to keep evil at bay.

An early and influential textbook was *The New England Primer*, first published in Boston in 1690 by Benjamin Harris. In the primer, children studied the alphabet, vowels, consonants, double letters, italic letters, italic double letters, capital letters, "easy" syllables, and then common words of many syllables.

A competing reader of the time was Noah Webster's *The Blue-*

Backed Speller, so named for its blue cover. Webster desired to rescue English from England, as it were. He rejected the study of Greek and Latin as prerequisites to English grammar. He argued for a language of the people and their ability to control it themselves, to embrace its fluidity, and to codify its differences from the mother tongue. Over time in his publications, Webster Americanized the British spelling of many words, for example, *defense, center, traveler, color.*

Webster makes an interesting observation about the shortcomings of other school readers for children: "Among the defects and absurdities found in the books of this kind hitherto used, we may rank the *want* of a thorough investigation of the sounds in the English language, and the powers of the several letters…and particularly the omission of a criterion by which the various sounds of the vowels may be distinguished."

In 1796 Horace Mann was born in Massachusetts. He would grow up to be the great reformer of American education. It was his opinion that schools should be available to everyone. He is truly the father of public-school education in the U.S. In *The Common School Journal*, which he founded and edited, Mann outlined the six principles of his reform in 1838: that the public needed to be saved from ignorance; that it was the public's obligation to pay for and sustain education; that schools should embrace children from all backgrounds; that education must be liberated from religious studies and should be non-sectarian; that education is a by-product of a free society; and that teachers must be professional and well-trained. He immediately called for the abolishment of corporal punishment as a school discipline. Mann organized a normal-school system later known as teachers' colleges. Mann's idea was that a common learning experience broached the divides of class and race. He called it a way to "equalize the conditions of men."

At the same time, schools farther west were developing their own materials. In 1833 Reverend William H. McGuffey created a series of books that became known as *The McGuffey Readers*, which focused

on morals and Christian religious belief. This was g
with discussions of civility, humanity, and social valu

Publishers affected the way that children read,
more important developments in early American educatio..
from men outside of commerce. The brilliant philosopher and psy-
chologist John Dewey also exerted lasting influence in education as
he pressed to humanize the rigid, often brutal classrooms of his day.
Beginning in 1897 and continuing through 1938, Dewey published a
series of theories on education that altered the way learning was ap-
proached in the classroom.

Dewey wished to reinvent the relationship between teacher and
student. He thought the teacher should not stand at the front of the
classroom spooning out information but that he should act as a fa-
cilitator and a guide to a child's learning. His progressive approach,
for example, eliminated alphabetic learning and drills. He also wanted
students to experience things as they learned rather than to merely
hear about ideas in the abstract.

Almost immediately, followers of Dewey took these ideas of
democratic relationships of teacher and students to extremes. Dewey became alarmed as pedagogues invoked his philosophies and created child-centered education that, he argued, gave the students too
much of the burden for their own education. Too much freedom
would be detrimental, Dewey countered. He wanted to ensure that
the role of the teacher not be minimized, but that it be focused on
the student's discovery of knowledge.

By the 1920s, U.S. educators gathered around two competing concepts of teaching reading. The more traditional one was that a student
learning to read should be taught the individual sounds that letters
and combinations of letters can make. Armed with these tools of the
finite sound combinations possible in the English language, a student
would be able to decode any word. This approach was known as learning by phonics. Phonics refers to the sounds of the spoken language

,ritten down, or, simply said, the sounds of English as represented by the letters of the alphabet.

The competing idea was that instead of teaching a student the component parts of a word and the accompanying rules that govern its sounds, a student who already speaks the language could be shown an entire word, recognize it, and add it to a list of known words, gradually amassing a vocabulary sufficient to read. This method became the whole-word, sight-word, or whole-language approach to reading.

By the 1930s and 1940s, many schools replaced a phonic-centered method with a look-say approach, that is, that a child would read familiar words until he or she could recognize them on sight. Students were supposed to gain reading skills through recognizing these whole words. When they read, "Run Spot, run. See Spot run," made famous by the William Scott Gray programs known to a generation as *Dick and Jane Readers*, students were to pick up common words and feel that they were readers. Educators believed that this gave students a jump start to reading. A student could see a word such as *run*, memorize the shape of its letters, and through repetition, gain a sense of accomplishment quickly.

In this scene of controversy, an important figure appeared who was doing interesting research. Dr. Samuel Orton, after receiving his medical degree from Harvard in 1906, worked in the departments of Neuropathology and Psychiatry at hospitals in Pennsylvania and Iowa. He became chairman of the Department of Psychiatry at the University of Iowa College of Medicine, and the founding director of the State Psychopathic Hospital in Iowa City, Iowa. In 1925, Orton organized a mobile unit, a sort of mental health clinic on wheels, in Greene County, Iowa. The goal of the unit was to speak to students whom teachers had referred because of troubles in school. These were students who were failing their classes and thought to be to mentally handicapped.

When Orton tested 14 of the students referred to him who couldn't read, they were found to have near-average, average, or above average

IQs. In Orton's travels with the mobile unit, he met a 16-year old who would change the course of Orton's life. Orton later wrote about the experience of meeting M. P., a person who "seemed bright but couldn't learn to read." M. P.'s troubles had nothing to do with intelligence.

This case opened up a world for Orton, and he made reading his life's work. In a groundbreaking article of 1925 titled, "Word Blindness in School Children," Orton published his study of M. P. He diagnosed the problem as physiological. The subject's brain was twisting and reversing the images of letters and making them unrecognizable as words. His term for the condition was strephosymbolia, which means twisted symbols. The condition had been observed for centuries in adults who suffered strokes, but also in children who had not had strokes. Dr. Rudolf Berlin of Stuttgart coined the term dyslexia in 1887 from the Greek "dys" (hard, bad, difficult) and "lexia" (word).

Orton's theories loom so large in reading education because, as others had before him, he removed the stigma of lack of intelligence from the challenges of reading. He theorized that children who had no evidence of any delay or abnormality until confronted with reading failed to devolve consistent dominance of one side of the brain over the other, leading to confusion and resulting in various forms of language disability. Over the next decades he developed remedial programs and, along with colleagues, created training systems that became the foundation for a modern, neurologically-based approach to teaching reading.

Orton became the director of the Language Research Project of the Neurological Institute of New York. His colleagues there were Paul Dozier, Edwin Cole, and Anna Gillingham. Along with Bessie Stillman, Gillingham created a training program for teaching reading based on Orton's work and made it applicable to the classroom. The key to the system was the connection of visual, auditory, and kinesthetic pathways to the brain. In reading, kinesthetics refers to the muscles of the mouth and arm. It was a multisensory approach, and it became known as the Orton-Gillingham method. Many other pro-grams developed from the Orton approach.

This is the backdrop of reading in America at the middle of the twentieth century. In 1955 Rudolf Flesch wrote a book that captured the undercurrent of discontent in reading education in the country. The book, *Why Johnny Can't Read*, was an indictment of the school system. And millions of people took notice.

By the mid-1950s, whole-word reading had supplanted phonics in most schools. The use of the whole-word method began the march toward the near-elimination of phonics instruction from American classrooms. This had a decidedly negative impact on many children's ability to learn to read. But that is but one-half of the equation. Once a child learns to read, these skills can be put to reading to learn about history, science, and the arts, opening up a whole world of knowledge.

Flesch's argument was that the two philosophical tracks of read-ing education were not parallel at all. In his view, one track was veer-ing off course into a dangerous place of illiteracy, and, unfortunately, in his view, it was the route most students traveled. Flesch wrote, "Ever since 1500 B.C.—whenever an alphabetic system of writing was used—people have learned to read by simply memorizing the sound of each letter in their alphabet. Except 20th-century America. We have thrown 3500 years of civilization out the window." *Why Johnny Can't Read* hit the bestseller lists and stayed there for more than 30 weeks, and it remained in print for decades and through multiple editions.

Flesch criticized the whole-word, or look-say, approach of the *Dick and Jane Readers* as having no research behind it to prove that it works. Because the teaching method dictated the content, Flesch maintained, the language of the *Dick and Jane* series ended up as "arti-ficial sequences of words—meaningless, stupid, totally uninteresting to a six-year-old child or anyone else."

The result of the ensuing debate was the inclusion of phonics in at least some new textbooks. But the educational establishment warned that the reintroduction of phonics to American classrooms would presage a return to rote memorization of what they felt were "meaningless sounds."

Eager for answers to these conflicting points of view, the Carnegie Corporation in 1961 called on Dr. Jeanne S. Chall of the Graduate School of Education at Harvard University to study the issue. Chall's extensive study had clear conclusions: while there was no one, optimum way to teach reading, the best results for *beginning reading* are obtained by using strategies that enable children to "break the code" of language—in other words, phonics. Armed with the ability to sound out words, children can more effectively recognize words and begin to read with understanding. Chall determined that programs that eschew phonics skip an essential first step toward literacy.

Chall's scholarship did not translate into a massive change in educational policy. For the vast majority of teachers in the 1960s, the whole-word method was in use. Chall herself warned of an overemphasis on phonics as a "magic bullet," lest this preferred teaching approach end up being blamed ten or twenty years down the road for whatever lack of success ensued. Rather, she preferred that phonics be stressed as a "beginning reading method." By warning that phonics could be blamed for possible shortcomings in instruction, the educational historian Diane Ravitch notes that Chall "described with canny accuracy the rise of the whole-language movement" in the 1980s.

The concept of whole-language is hard to pin down exactly. Some of it was based on a false application of Gestalt psychology which posited studying the whole person in the whole environment. Theorist Kenneth Goodman stated, "Whole-language learning builds around whole learners learning whole-language in whole situations." Methods that "chop language into bits and pieces," i.e., phonics instruction, are to be avoided, he wrote.

Such was the case in California, when a whole-language reading curriculum was put in place in 1987. A half-decade later, the extent of the academic disaster became clear when the National Assessment of

Educational Progress began administering tests on a state-by-state basis. California finished a dismal fourth from the bottom in reading, ahead of Mississippi, Washington, D.C., and Guam. Two years later, even Mississippi pulled ahead of the Golden State.

In 1997 Congress asked the Director of the National Institute of Child Health and Human Development, in consultation with the Secretary of Education, to convene a national panel to assess the status of research-based knowledge, including the effectiveness of various approaches to teaching children to read. A distinguished National Reading Panel was assembled and a landmark report was published in 2000 titled, "Teaching Children to Read: An Evidence-Based Assessment of the Scientific Research Literature on Reading and Its Implications for Reading Instruction." It supported phonics instruction incontrovertibly. The report had examined 373 relevant studies. It stated: "The meta-analysis indicated that systematic phonics instruction enhances children's success in learning to read and that systematic phonics instruction is significantly more effective than instruction that teaches little or no phonics."

Teaching reading continues to spark controversy. The only losers in this battle are the children, who continue to lag behind as adults bicker over what should no longer be points of debate.

We constantly hear of the changing nature of society and technology. There is no question that the advent of the Internet and widespread availability of computers linked together through wireless connections has, and will continue to have a profound effect on education. As newspapers and magazines struggle, victims of the glut of information available online, it certainly is appropriate to question how this will have an effect on teaching, learning, and reading. But when it comes to learning to read, these technological advances only make learning to read, and later, reading more complicated material, even more important. The world already belongs to the literate. In the future, reading skills will be even more essential to success in an information-based society.

What should be clear from this little overview of history is that reading skills will never be unimportant in the future. Whatever technological change is occurring, and whatever change will occur in the future that we cannot conceive of today, one thing is certain: children will need to learn to read and write if they are to be successful, both in school and in life.

CHAPTER III

Recognizing the Problem and Organizing to Meet It

AS TEACHERS GRADUATE FROM COLLEGE AND GRADUATE SCHOOL, very few have even heard of Orton or of similar methodologies. Teachers are not taught *how* to teach reading, *how* to teach writing, *how* to teach spelling, *how* to teach comprehension, *how* to teach mathematics, history, geography or science. A study done in 2006 by the National Council on Teacher Quality (see appendix) revealed that only 15% of the education institutions studied taught all the components of the science of reading, which include phonetic awareness, phonics, fluency, vocabulary and comprehension.

After graduating, the young teachers go into the classroom. They are eager and bright-eyed. They discover that their students simply aren't learning to read. Imagine their frustration. Some of these fine teachers burn out. A few ask other teachers if there is anything else out there. They are searching for solutions. That's when, typically, they call Reading Reform Foundation of New York.

Reading Reform Foundation of New York was founded in 1979, when a group of teachers from the New York City area met at an out-of-town symposium on reading, and they began to talk with one another. Of this band of educators, two teachers dealt with children with learning problems; two more taught in the New York City public schools; one taught adult former offenders in the justice system; and one was an engineer who ran a tutoring business. All agreed that there was no acceptable reason that huge numbers of children couldn't read. Back at home, a series of phone calls ensued and then a first meeting, which was held at the Fortune Society where Peggy Bishop, the adult literacy teacher, welcomed the group.

The teachers who met at the historic conference in 1979 were all working with different types of students, both children and adults. They were curious to discover the unifying practices that enabled them all to succeed as reading professionals.

They found that they had three specific things in common. First, all had found mentors, and they had sought training or figured out on their own how to represent to students the sounds of the English language in logical ways. They all taught that letters of the alphabet, as well as groups of letters in English, represented most of the sounds of English, such as *igh*, which always says *i*. They all had found a way to teach phonics systematically, building each day on the previous day's lesson.

Second, all of them believed that students must be taught to put these sounds into words: short words first, then multisyllabic words. Furthermore, students must be taught to simultaneously write and say the sounds and the words as they were learning them. This kind of approach is called multisensory teaching. Writing the sounds while seeing them on cards or on the board, using the muscles of the mouth to pronounce and the muscles of the arm to write, as well as hearing the teacher and other students saying the sounds, uses many pathways to the brain. Each sensory pathway helps reinforce the others, making learning easier.

Finally, they were all in agreement that when students learn to write the sounds and words from dictation, they are ready to begin to read simple books at first, then increasingly more difficult ones.

Four of the group were fortunate enough to find mentors who had been trained in the Orton approach. Peggy Bishop had struggled with reading until, in her 30's, she discovered phonics and developed a program called *The ABCs and All Their Tricks* that she used successfully with adults. The engineer in the group, Charles Richardson, had put his wife's methods of teaching reading on machines that he developed himself decades before anyone else did. Two members, Sylvia Goldsmith and Emily Goldberg, had been trained in and worked with the Orton approach for many years as developmental reading consultants in private practice. Rena Stanford was a public-school teacher also trained in an Orton method. Sandra Priest Rose had studied with Romalda Spalding, a disciple of Dr. Orton, who had devised on her own a method based on his research.

Fortuitously, a lawyer named Sidney Korzenik, a resident of an upper-income suburban community, also attended this formative meeting. He had observed that his own children in their prestigious local public school were being taught reading in an "illogical way," and he had undertaken the task of teaching them himself. It was he who, within the first two years of the group's meeting, sought incorporation of the organization as a not-for-profit charity that would eventually become Reading Reform Foundation of New York. A Board of Trustees was formed whose members would shape the direction of the organization over the next thirty years.

Sharpening the Focus; Shaping the Direction

In those early years the Reading Reform Foundation founders set goals that were ambitious but attainable. They thought of themselves as a resource for teachers. Their activities highlighted the desire to make information available to teachers rather than some larger movement to redefine what reading education should be. From the beginning they shied away from policy-making. It seemed to them then—and it has remained a key tenet now—that ultimately they would have more impact on education if they educated educators by being hands-on trainers.

The two initial areas of work were training courses and workshops given at the Reading Reform Foundation headquarters, and an annual conference for professional teachers and administrators.

At first, these courses were held in a tiny, rented office on West 57th Street in Manhattan. Later, because of an encouraging response, Reading Reform expanded the workshops into a larger space at the same location. Subsidies from friends and supporters enabled these courses to be affordable to those enrolled. The fact that teachers were willing to spend their own limited resources of time and money for professional development demonstrated that Reading Reform Foundation had identified an important need. Advertisements in the United Federation of Teachers newspaper brought in many teachers. Teachers, in turn, told their principals about the courses they had spent their own money to take. Over the past thirty years, more than 6,000 teachers have taken the courses.

The Annual Conference

A retired teacher, Leona Spector, and her husband Philip, came to the first Reading Reform Foundation conference, held in 1981. Immediately, they volunteered their services to run future conferences. Under their expertise this annual gathering grew in scope, subject matter, and resourcefulness. Beginning with 100 attendees, it attracted up to 600 attendees annually over the next 26 years. More than 14,000 teachers have attended the conferences.

At the conferences, keynote speakers from a broad range of professions discussed significant issues regarding reading and literacy. Most of these speakers were from the world of education, but others hailed from completely different fields. All felt passionately about reading, such as Isaac Asimov, Arthur Ashe, Leon Botstein, Bob Kerrey, and Frank McCourt. Other keynote speakers and those who presented papers and gave workshop presentations included city government officials, university professors, magazine editors, non-fiction authors, museum directors, pediatric specialists, astrophysicists, theater directors, reading experts, children's book writers, heads of private schools, and New York State regents.

The conferences helped spark the growth of the organization. The conferences provided workshop sessions, panels, speakers, and book publisher exhibits. Every attendee was greeted personally by Reading Reform Foundation volunteers and helped throughout the conference day. Classroom teachers enjoyed the day and the lunch hugely. Reading Reform Foundation Board members and others volunteered to chair workshops, staff information desks, and affix signs to identify workshop rooms.

The In-School Teacher-Training Program Develops

The program of training teachers in the schools started with two members of the Board of Trustees, Sylvia Goldsmith and Emily Goldberg. They went into a school to demonstrate the program to teachers. At the same time, in 1985, two public-school teachers asked Reading Reform Foundation to come into their school. The teachers had attended one of their courses, and they wanted someone to model in an actual classroom what they had learned. This was an important moment in the history of the organization because it revealed what was necessary to accomplish the organization's goals. It is one thing to present ideas in the abstract; it is quite another to hammer out details in the real world.

As the initial trainers modeled an approach to reading in the school, it became apparent that most teachers are expected to teach reading, writing, and spelling without ever having taken a course that effectively taught them how to do it. They struggled. It had nothing to do with their abilities as teachers. And certainly it was not a question of desire to be excellent teachers. The only thing they lacked was a solid approach that worked. Many generations of teachers, for example, are unaware that in the English language, spelling and pronunciation are both logical and predictable. Imagine what a difference that single concept makes for a teacher.

What began as a small program offering courses of instruction soon grew into an intense, year-long collaboration between Reading Reform Foundation teaching consultants and classroom teachers. These initial experiences in the classroom pointed the organization to a long-range plan. It realized that it needed to work within the system. The involvement of the principal was paramount. The organization was in a school at the principal's invitation. For teachers to become self-sufficient, twice-a-week mentoring visits were essential to help develop lesson plans, to practice the material concept by concept, and to enhance the teacher's technique and delivery through repetition and steady monitoring. Planning sessions took place before class time, after which the Reading Reform consultant remained in the classroom while the teacher delivered the material and interacted with the students. As needed, the consultants would provide coaching by interjecting an idea or two, sometimes supplementing a teacher's comment with an on-the-spot demonstration. Each teacher appreciated the hands-on support and guidance. But the consultant always kept in mind that this was not her classroom; it was the teacher's. The mentor was there to help; that balance of expertise and respect became a bedrock principle of the organization.

The Foundation's courses needed to be shaped to the realities and challenges of the inner-city classroom. It needed to be flexible enough to help classroom teachers to accommodate students who were learning English and who had varying levels of parental support at home. These factors affected the students and had to be considered as the organization developed its approach to teaching reading in the inner-city public schools. Those initial classroom experiences helped Reading Reform Foundation to evolve and standardize both the work in the classroom as well as the necessary groundwork to be invited into the classroom in the first place. The program quickly expanded and more trainers were added in those first years.

The Organization's Structure Develops

The founders of Reading Reform Foundation made five key observations: the organization needed an executive director and a director of program/curriculum; the training of consultants needed to be systematic and comprehensive in order for them to feel confident enough to mentor; the school's principal had to be firmly on board in order for the training to succeed, and the program needed to be supervised closely. Esther Morgan Sands was one of the first Reading Reform consultants in the schools, and it became apparent that she should continue as a consultant but also had the qualifications to supervise others.

Today Reading Reform Foundation's executive director, Lauren Wedeles, and Esther Morgan Sands, director of program and curriculum, are the links to the school principals that give meaning and substance to the program. Their meetings with new and old principals provide the feeling of collegiality and cooperation that Reading Reform Foundation always has sought to establish.

Lauren Wedeles, in addition to writing grant proposals to foundations, supervising applications for public funds, overseeing all the financial and program recordkeeping of the organization and being involved in all policy-making, is the person whom the schools call on personnel and budgetary problems.

It's no surprise to learn that public schools have limited funds for new programs. At first, Reading Reform Foundation charged the schools only 10% of the expense of running the program in the schools, covering the costs of materials and staffing. Eventually, the percentage was increased to a 20% charge. Reading Reform Foundation worked diligently to raise the rest from public and private sources. Fundraising, grant writing, an annual Benefit, and, well, polite begging became necessary tools that enabled the work to flourish.

Esther Morgan Sands works closely with the principals on setting up schedules for twice-a-week preparation periods and training in the classroom. She makes sure things run smoothly during the school year, observing whether the teaching consultants and the classroom teachers are compatible, ironing out problems and seeing that lessons proceed well. Once the program is set up in each school, she logs in hundreds of miles and countless hours traveling to each of the 25 schools and 75 classrooms where Reading Reform Foundation is at work.

Supervision is essential and integral to the program. It is one of the secrets of success each year. Problems are handled immediately and not allowed to fester. Esther Sands visits each of the 35 consultants in the schools a minimum of twice a semester. Two assistant supervisors, Charlotte Haber and Judith Muniz, visit twice a semester also. They help when there are trouble spots and can report to the program director, who then decides if her help is needed. Teaching consultants are encouraged also to telephone the director if there are any problems. This sometimes takes up to two or three hours nightly for Esther Sands.

Lauren and Esther are the public face of the organization to all the schools served, the organizations and the individuals that fund the Foundation. Their integrity, loyalty and passion have built the program from two to 75 classrooms per year and have resulted in respect for and influence of this small organization far beyond its immediate reach. Teachers whose students have been taught in earlier grades with the programs of Reading Reform Foundation often request that the organization come to their classes too, after they see that the Reading Reform students know so much and can attack new words with ease.

When the training program began, all of the consultants were experienced in using an Orton approach, but as new consultants were added, there was a need to develop a unified training system for them. The organization developed a year-long associates program for people who wanted to become consultants. The public-school teachers would need a 40- to 45-hour course in order to use the program, and so would the consultants. For time-strapped school teachers and consultants, this would be an enormous commitment.

There is value to the introductory training course for classroom teachers being held in the Reading Reform office: a professional approach is established; there are no distractions; promptness is required. No food is permitted during lecture time but there are regular coffee and lunch breaks.

After taking a course, the trainee/consultant shadows one of the Reading Reform Foundation consultants already on staff for an entire year. The trainee needs to see not only how material is delivered, but how diplomatic the consultants are with everyone in the school and in the classroom. At the end of the school year, the trainee retakes the week-long course. Now, having had the experience of the classroom, the course has newfound meaning. After this, the trainee is eligible to mentor new classroom teachers on her own.

Reading Reform mentor demonstrating spelling
technique with the classroom teacher

CHAPTER IV

The Teaching of Teachers

THEY ARE GATHERED IN A MEDIUM-SIZED ROOM IN THE MIDDLE of Manhattan. A few blocks away from Central Park, thirty-five women sit in chairs with arms attached to write on. The room is at street level in an Art Deco building constructed nearly 70 years ago, with residential apartments overhead and offices on the first floor. Passersby on the sidewalk scurry about on a warm spring day while the people inside concentrate on the tasks at hand. Although the metal and laminate seats aren't very comfortable, the women are obviously comfortable with each other. There is a gentle buzz of camaraderie in the room. They are laughing, joking, and smiling. They compare notes of their experiences as trainers for Reading Reform Foundation of New York, and they are having one of their monthly meetings in their offices in Midtown. Over sandwiches, they enjoy each other's company throughout a three-hour session.

The women have been gathering regularly for years. There is a small degree of turnover, and many of them have been Reading Reform Foundation mentors for a long time. Nearly all of the trainers are retired school teachers. They understand the public school system inside and out. One would imagine that they would be jaded about teaching and burnt out by now, but the opposite appears to be true: they revel in every success no matter how small it first appears.

Among themselves they share stories of recent encounters in the schools as trainers for Reading Reform Foundation. Bette Kessler, who currently works with a school in Brooklyn, relates an exchange she had when she worked with students from East New York, one of the city's neighborhoods most vexed by poverty and crime. She tells of a little boy in second grade who didn't want to learn to read. He wore a scarf that signified he was already in a gang. As she tried to help him in school, he said he didn't need to learn how to read. When Bette asked him the reason, he replied that he already knew what he was going to be: a pimp. She didn't flinch. Instead, she laid out an argument for pimp literacy, so to speak. Pimps have to write contracts, she countered, and they have to read to do their jobs. And she continued and outlined all of the reasons a second-grade gangster wanting to be a pimp needed education in order to be successful. She didn't back down, and slowly the little boy blossomed into a wonderful student. At the end of the year, the same little boy slipped a note to Bette, "Thanks for teaching me sight words and suffixes. And when you die, a piece of you will break off and go into my heart."

The teaching of reading in our schools is not about a tug-of-war between methodologies. Ultimately, it has little to do with ideologies, politics, even its own history. Teaching is about the students—how to reach each of them, how to prepare them, how to challenge them, and how to engage them. It becomes clear, observing this casual meeting in a classroom-like space in midtown, that each of these trainers devotes herself to this mission.

The Heart of the Program: In-Class Mentoring

The training consultants form the heart of the program. Their expertise, delivered in a caring, warm, non-judgmental, collegial way to the classroom teacher, is the backbone of the success of the program. Most of the consultants have spent years in the public schools themselves and know the pressures and strains on classroom teachers. Now retired, they are proud of their roles in helping teachers and children succeed. Their twice-a-week visits are greeted with smiles from the children and teachers alike. The 40-minute preparation period preceding each classroom visit is a time to iron out problems from past lessons, plan new lessons, and practice how to deliver the lessons smoothly. It is sometimes a time for confidences about life problems given to a friendly ear as they plan together. The consultants are there as professionals who try to be supportive in every way possible.

After the preparation period the consultants go into the classroom with the teacher to demonstrate and model lessons at first, but gradually as the year goes on, they do less and less so that the classroom teacher really takes over. The consultant gets to know all the children too and can observe when extra help is needed. Consultants also bear an additional burden of bringing in pencils, paper, tests and books for the children and teaching materials for the teacher. They are all good-natured about it. As the children finish one reader, consultants have to return them to the Foundation's rotating library and then bring in new sets of books for two to four classrooms.

The letters of thanks and love at the end of the year from children make the hard work of the consultants worthwhile. They know they have started from 50 to 100 children per year on a road to academic and life success.

It can be daunting for the newly trained classroom teacher to be faced in the fall with using an Orton mode of teaching alone, without the warm, helpful support of her mentor of the previous year. He or she may be afraid to embark alone on something new. Therefore, the Foundation devised its Jump-Start sessions, made available to the classroom teacher trained the previous school year. The consultant who trained the teacher comes in to visit the teacher once or twice early in the new school year to help get the program started, re-establish contact and give encouragement. These sessions have proven to be valuable in ensuring that the hard work of training is not lost.

The obvious question about this success versus the dreary realities of education in much of America is this: if such phonetic, multisensory methods are so terrific, why aren't they taught everywhere?

Reading Reform Foundation of New York chooses not to be the muckrakers on the issue, however passionately they feel about it. Suffice it to say that the market forces at work are tremendous and pervasive. There are educational consultants, contracts with publishers, paid programs from companies large and small—each of which is a contributing factor. At the very least, few teachers are taught such an approach in their training to be educators.

The Role of Principals

The involvement of the school principal is essential to the success of the program. He or she must be on board whole-heartedly to make the intensive training work. After the principal has met with the Reading Reform Foundation executive director and the director of program and curriculum, who explain the program, the principal selects two classroom teachers to be trained. Often, teachers volunteer to be trained. This is quite a commitment because it requires taking a 40- or 45-hour course in the summer before the school year and then voluntarily giving up two preparation periods a week to plan lessons and practice with the Foundation's reading consultants.

Two to four teachers are usually asked to participate. Essentially, it is a "bottom-up" philosophy. If two teachers become enthusiastic about the program the first year, they will often encourage their
peers to sign on for the second year, and by the third year, entire
grades might be participating. The principal works out a schedule
with the Foundation's program director for the two preparation periods per week for lesson planning alongside the consultant. This is
followed by in-class modeling and demonstration. By mid-year, the
classroom teacher generally takes over the lessons, with the consultant playing a supportive role.

The Reading Reform consultant visits 60 times during the school
year. NO OTHER ORGANIZATION IN THE COUNTRY HAS THIS KIND
OF CONTINUOUS AND FOLLOW-UP TRAINING. The goal is to leave
a well-trained teacher who can use this approach with any curriculum
for the rest of his or her professional life.

It would be remiss not to praise the hundreds of principals who
have embraced the Reading Reform approach over the years. They
are dedicated and extremely hard-working professionals. Most of
these schools are in inner-city areas where the principals are called
upon to be instructional leaders, masters of budget-making, leaders
in communities in which their schools are located, and counselors to
teachers and parents who are facing extraordinary problems and con-
cerns. Additionally, these principals have the onerous tasks of nego-
tiating their way through a mine-field of directives from on high in a
tense environment that is constantly changing. The principals manage all of this with a combination of strong leadership, empathy, and
much-needed good humor. These principals who labor in the school
vineyards are to be saluted.

Writing is an essential component of learning to read.

CHAPTER V

A Logical Approach to Teaching Reading, Writing, Spelling and Comprehension

THE MOMENT WHEN WE START TO LEARN TO READ—BUT THE issue is larger than reading because it includes writing and spelling and reasoning too—is worth exploring a bit more because so much is at stake. The degree to which children begin to master literacy sets up many landmarks of success in their lives. Conversely, a failure to master them creates monumental roadblocks.

The complications of a child learning to read and write spring from this simple statement: human brains are hard-wired to speak, but not to read and write. We acquire language-speaking skills in completely different ways from that of the ability to translate language to a series of graphic symbols. Even further removed is the ability to conform to a system of writing that is the same as everyone else who uses the language, which itself has a long and complex history of mutation, annexation, and evolution. Theoretically, as far as the brain is concerned, everyone could speak the language without being able to write a sentence that others could decode.

The process of decoding is what early education is all about. It feels odd to a young child to have to learn a language they already know, but our world requires it; otherwise, we are verbal without being literate.

There are six stages of reading skill development, according to Jeanne Chall, former director of the Reading Laboratory at Harvard University. Chall writes that as we develop, we move through each level, paraphrased below (*The Reading Crisis: Why Poor Children Fall Behind*).

STAGE 0 is a period of prereading. The child is exposed to words in print as he looks at his environment, at street signs, advertisements, and even cereal boxes and television commercials.

STAGE 1 is a phase in which the child recognizes the principle of the alphabet, that is, that the letters of the alphabet correspond to specific sounds of speech.

STAGE 2 is a period of expansion and consolidation of the above principle. Ultimately, the child masters the written rules of language to such an extent that reading becomes automatic.

STAGE 3 marks the beginning of advanced skills of learning and thinking. As Chall writes, "...you are no longer learning to read, you are reading to learn."

STAGES 4 and 5 involve higher levels of reasoning that use reading as a springboard to compare theories and opposing points of view.

How does a child learn to read, write and spell? Specifically, as a child begins school, what should come first?

This is a theoretical question that draws from the studies of how a brain learns things about language and literacy, and it is tempered with practical issues drawn from the experience of educators who have tried many different approaches to maximize learning.

Reading Reform Foundation of New York's success is based on science via the studies of Dr. Samuel T. Orton on neural functioning. The nuts and bolts of the process of teaching come from programs such as Orton-Gillingham that make Orton's studies practical for teachers in schools. Another Orton program was developed by Romalda Bishop Spalding, who devised a method described in her book, *The Writing Road to Reading*, initially appearing in 1957. Also using the Orton-Gillingham approach, Esther Sands developed cards based on the work of Aylett Cox and Sally Childs.

The first important lesson is that letters of the alphabet correspond to the sounds of speech, either as individual letters or as letter combinations. These letter pairings are called phonograms (the word phonogram comes from two Greek words, *phono*, sound, and *gram*, writing: that is, sounds written down). Despite the vast possibilities of words and sounds that can be derived from our 26-letter alphabet, the number of phonograms is relatively finite and knowable. There are approximately 70 basic phonograms. They are derived from the letters of the alphabet plus the combinations of two, three, and four letters put together that make one sound, such as *ea, ng,* and *ough.* The philosophy of the Orton-based approaches is that a young student can master the phonograms and store that information in memory to build a sample of most of the written units possible in the English language.

This is not a long, tortured process to learn. If done methodically and clearly, phonogram acquisition and mastery happens quickly, after which students begin reading, writing and spelling almost immediately. Furthermore, these phonograms will serve the students throughout their lives just as the rules of spelling help them to decipher any word thrown at them. It also aids in retention of new words and an understanding of their origin and meaning. The understanding of words—their meaning, yes, but also their origin and their connections to cultures and history—is a natural bridge to more advanced analysis of the written word and the ideas they seek to represent.

Note the importance of seeing, saying, hearing, and writing simultaneously. This is called multisensory teaching. It is also multisensory learning. Students hear the teacher say a word. They say it aloud in response. They hear it being said. They write a word. They use muscles of the hand. They feel it being written. They see the word written down. All of these senses come into play to reinforce concepts in the brain. This multisensory approach is especially powerful when you consider that each student learns differently and has disparate innate strengths. By engaging all of the senses together in an action as simple as writing and saying a word, one's weaknesses are compensated by one's strengths. Someone who is a "visual learner," for example, can easily lean on that process; conversely, someone who learns better by hearing can learn by hearing everyone in the class recite together. These are only two examples. Every student has specific ways to best access new information. A multisensory approach practically guarantees the best results. This approach employs four sensory channels to the mind: hearing, saying, writing, and seeing. Similarly, this method has been shown to be exceptionally effective with pupils who are learning English as a second language and students with learning disabilities.

At first, the precision of the method might appear to be something of a surprise for young children and for their teachers. Suddenly, language is broken down in logical ways that they never considered before. It is not a barrier, but a gateway. It is a necessary step for a young child to examine language closely rather than simply memorizing a few easy words, and then learning a few more. Students need a logical way to learn thousands of words. This must be done systematically because active learning of a writing and reading system compensates for the brain's inability to soak it up innately. There is another even more basic reason for learning in this way: the child already knows how to speak; what he or she needs is to learn how to read, write and spell. These are separate and unfamiliar tasks.

Adults who have never looked at the rules of language tend to think that English is messy, confusing, and unregulated. They would be surprised to walk into a first-grade class that has been studying using an Orton approach for only a few months. Here are children who can recite rules with ease, but, even more importantly, have used the rules as a governing system to make sense of their language.

Spelling

In the beginning a kindergarten classroom is not a level playing field. To address the children's differences in exposure to the written and spoken word on the first day of school, the Reading Reform program creates a common ground, and it enables the teacher to bring everyone together to focus on new skills. One of the first tasks is to present the sounds of language in written form. The classroom teacher introduces students to single letters and then to groups of letters. The teacher has a stack of cards that are printed large enough so that the entire class can read them from a distance.

The Sands cards have a simple picture and a letter on the card: for example, the letter *g* and a picture of chewing gum. The card is presented to the class and the teacher models the hard sound of the *g g.* The children repeat, "Gum, *g.*" In another method, the students sound out the letter *g* without a picture. That is, they say, *g,* a hard, gutteral sound. In both approaches, the children master the sounds of every letter of the alphabet and then the groups of letters that make one sound in English. These sounds in their written form are called phonograms.

Going through the sounds of the letters is a morning drill. Students complete it rapidly. As the students become sure of a phonogram, that card is deleted from the stack. The students also begin to learn the rules associated with each phonogram. For example, the card for the phonogram *qu* includes an explanation that in English *q* is always followed by the letter *u* in a word.

The majority of the phonograms—roughly two thirds—have only one sound. Eleven phonograms have two sounds, and ten have three sounds. There are six different ways to pronounce the phonogram *ough* (in Spalding, examples are *though, through, rough, cough, thought, and bough*). As the class learns the basic phonograms, they also discover the rules that apply to them, and they master words composed of phonograms.

After a few basic letters are taught, a class presentation goes something like the following: the teacher presents a word to the class by saying it and putting it in a sentence. Then she asks the children to speak the first sound of that word. The children give the first sound and write it and continue, sound by sound. Eventually, they can do this with syllables. They write down the first syllable, and the teacher writes it on the board. The teacher continues with the next syllable of the word, systematically proceeding until all of the syllables are identified, spoken, and written down. The appropriate spelling rules are invoked with each word.

The class works in unison. Said another way, the teacher does not single out a student for the correct answer to questions while those who don't know the answer hide silently and hope that their ignorance will not turn into embarrassment. Instead, everybody repeats the sounds or the rules aloud, at the same time, something like a combined chorus of knowledge. This is significant, particularly in the beginning, because the students who are slightly ahead of their peers in one concept or another bolster the entire class. The students who need more help get up to speed. Their confidence is not shaken. They are not marginalized, and they naturally get in the habit of full participation. This is how a class becomes completely engaged. By connecting to each other, they gain stability and strength. At the same time, the teacher can see weaknesses and can move to compensate for problems. This process of ramping up to a common threshold of literacy happens quickly.

Soon the students are spelling and writing. They learn approximately 29 rules of spelling. In the Spalding approach, for example, there are five possible reasons why a silent *e* is attached to the end of a word. Beginning students learn these rules speedily as they appear in words. It might seem a bit laborious for such young children to parse the inner-workings of language so soon, but actually, it is a liberating and energizing moment. Armed with a tool such as a spelling rule, the students begin to see examples of it everywhere they go. Once the students have learned 70 phonograms and some two dozen rules, they can spell approximately 87% of the words in English. Think of that: 87% of all of the words in our language are firmly in their grasp! It is not much of an exaggeration to say that such very young children have the entire language opened wide to them.

Teachers have the students keep a notebook of all the spelling words that they learn. The children amass an impressive personal reference volume. First graders learn new words at a rapid pace of even up to 30 words a week.

It is a challenge for teachers to explain to a student how a word can be understood. For a young person, a word is simply a string of letters. It is difficult for them to see how a word breaks down into segments. The phonograms are of great use here because they provide immediately recognizable clues to the decoding of words. The students have learned the basic phonograms and have written them and identified them in words. When they're writing, they are analyzing phonograms and applicable spelling rules.

The students build skills by adding new letters in combinations. They begin to recognize a group of letters that they already know in a new context. Then they see that the letters around it can change how it is pronounced and spelled. For example, they see the word *cat*. Having already learned the alphabet and the sounds letters make, they see and then write the components of the word: *c, aa, t, cat!* The teacher helps them put it all together, and they say the word, often with a surprised voice. Ah-ha! It is a word that they've heard before; they simply didn't know how it was supposed to be spelled.

As they learn to spell, the class uses a marking system to highlight phonograms, and in one method, prefixes and suffixes. They underline letters that go together. This shows them at a glance that the letters are a unit. Learning the sounds of letters and groups of letters as well as the spelling rules, the students identify words, and more importantly, they understand why they are structured and spelled as they are.

These methods to teach spelling, reading and writing drew from Dr. Orton's ideas of the functions of the brain and then made a system that could be used in school classrooms. When students walk into school the first day, they already speak the language. They typically have a few thousand words at their command. The process of writing words on paper is a magical moment. It is a window that lets the words in a child's brain flow in a completely new way.

Essentially, students learn how to document the sounds they speak. There is a strong kinesthetic connection between the muscles used to write down a word and to say it. Orton's success was tapping into the connection between muscle groups and the body's senses.

A very common learning handicap for young students is a tendency to reverse or confuse the sequence of letters as they write. Many children are born with this predisposition. If it isn't addressed, the problem can grow more and more frustrating and impede learning. Basically, it's an issue of left-to-right ordering. Some children innately want to go right to left. The confusion of order appears with individual letters as well as words. Many children flip letters upside down—the *p* becomes a *b*, for example, or reverse it—the *b* becomes a *d*. The problem is compounded if these students have to look over their shoulders while sitting at circular tables to see the blackboard. For them, it is like writing by looking into a mirror and trying to replicate the word on paper. Therefore it is preferable for the students to face the front of the classroom for reading, writing, and spelling. The act of writing reinforces the important left-to-right direction of seeing and reading properly.

Handwriting

There is one skill that is in some danger because of neglect. It is handwriting. We have become a world of typists. We spend most of our workday in front of a computer with a keyboard. We send email and text messages instead of picking up a telephone and certainly instead of picking up a pen. That's simply a fact of modern life. For many children, even the youngest, typing has replaced writing in their development as well. Whether this is a good thing or a bad thing is yet to be fully studied. Certainly, children at increasingly younger ages are exposed to books through technology. It offers some advantages. From a learning vantage point, however, this evolution of literacy, specifically how a word gets on a page or on a computer screen, has consequences.

Typing is not the same as writing. Particularly from a mental development standpoint, the pressing of letters on a keyboard is something like a shortcut or a detour. But unlike that traveling analogy, although the end result may look the same, it is the journey that is responsible for development, and shortcuts may cause more problems than they solve. The issue is not solely about a generation whose handwriting is sort of illegible; handwriting flows into spelling, which in turn predicts reading ability. The jury is out on the extent to which bypassing penmanship causes long-term negative consequences in learning. The problem—if it is a problem—is compounded by reading programs in schools that employ multimedia technology to teach literacy skills. Conceivably, some students in the country are learning to read, spell, and write entirely on electronic equipment. Is this progress if they cannot write legibly when the equipment fails?

As a reader, you may have forgotten exactly how you learned to read. If so, probably it is equally hard to remember how you learned to write. The methods used by Reading Reform Foundation are specific on the formation of letters and other details of writing. The process works as cleanly as it does for learning to decode letters and words in reading. And the bottom line is that it works.

The first considerations are creating an environment that is best for writing. Students clear their desks of clutter and any distracting materials that aren't needed for the task of writing. They sit in a physical position that promotes concentration—feet flat on the floor, hips against the back of their chairs, backs straight, heads are lifted up tall.

Why so specific? Does a student's body position really matter that much? What matters is that the child is sitting in a sustainable position. If he slouches forward, if his head droops down, if he is physically uncomfortable and fidgeting all about, he will not be able to focus as well, and writing will be a tiring, uphill battle. Just as mastering the recognition of phonograms was a prerequisite to spelling, correct and

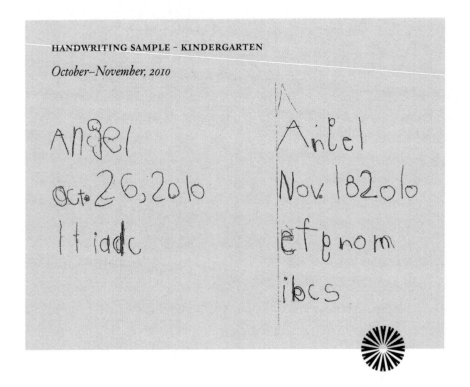

HANDWRITING SAMPLE - KINDERGARTEN

October–November, 2010

sustainable posture, hand position and paper placement all translate to ease and success for students as they begin to write.

As for the hand's position in holding a pencil, it's a relatively simple concept, but it takes a bit of getting used to. Every position is calibrated for control and also for ease. It does no one any good to hold the pencil in a way that makes the hand cramp. The child should hold the pencil where it is sharpened, resting between the first and second knuckle of the finger. The sensation of writing should be relaxed. Pressure in the arm and fingers should be minimized as much as possible. Students use wide, lined paper. First they learn to print. In second or third grade, they simply connect the letters to write in cursive.

There is a mistake that many parents and even some teachers make regarding children who are learning to write their letters. They fail to encourage children to get it right from the beginning. Consequently,

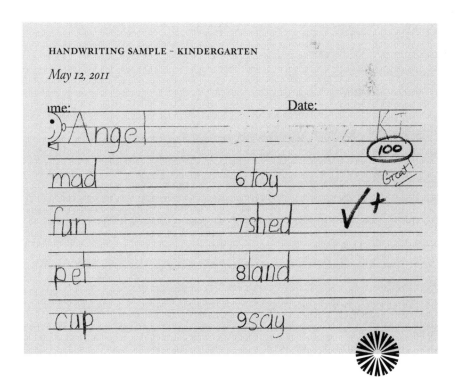

children get into habits of writing sloppily. Incorrectly-written letters affect children's ability to decipher them. There is a relationship between seeing correct symbols and translating them into sounds.

The shapes of the letters themselves, though varied, is relatively simple to teach children. All of the shapes of our alphabet's letters are based on five simple motions: a circle, a short vertical line, a long vertical line that extends up, a long vertical line that extends down, a slanting line, a horizontal dash. That's basically it.

Reading Reform Foundation teachers use a clock face to illustrate letters based on the circle. They ask students to imagine a clock with four numbers: 2, 4, 8, and 10. The letter *c*, for example, begins at 2 and then counterclockwise ends at 4. That is a *c*. Other letters that begin at 2 on the clock face are *a, d, f, g, o, s,* and *q*. The majority of letters are straight-line letters that start at the top or middle and sit on the line. Children also learn capital letters and numbers at the same time. All of this instruction—perhaps not mastery, but that will come with practice—generally proceeds quickly and almost effortlessly.

Vocabulary

The Reading Reform lesson is not all drill in spelling rules, nor syllable division. It also can be used to find the root meanings of words and to analyze the words for their meaning.

Hence, in a classroom in the Parker Elementary School in Mount Vernon, New York, the student composition of which is similar to many inner-city classrooms, the children are writing vocabulary with their teacher, Celestine Garner. She is working closely with her mentor, Bonnie Lee Apple. The two clearly enjoy working together.

After the rapid morning drill with phonogram cards, which have no pictures in this case because these are the Spalding cards, the children proceed to the vocabulary that is part of the program. They write and analyze the words "soon" and "came," followed by the word "Sunday," pronounced clearly by the teacher. She puts the word into a sentence. Then she asks in syllables, "What do you think Sun day is named for?" A chorus of voices calls out, "The sun?" "Yes!" the teacher says, and so the careful writing begins, syllable by syllable. "And then, what do you think Mon day is named for?", with a drawn-out emphasis pronounced on the "Mon." Excited discovery produces a chorus of, "the moon?" "Yes! It is the moon's day."

Here the power and fascination of words and meanings are made palpable in a first-grade class in a district replete with many social and economic problems. These children are being introduced to an intellectual way of thinking.

Reading

After these basics are in place, reading begins. Reading Reform Foundation starts with simple primers at first, and quickly the children yearn for more. Reading, as it turns out, isn't all about rules and decoding after all. It is about ideas, reasoning, and exploration. The first day that students begin to read, even with simple primers, they can focus on content. They think about it. They talk about what they've read with peers and mentors. Using their spelling skills, they decode words more easily, and this allows them to read for other purposes than to wrestle new words to the ground. They start reasoning right away. These thought processes are all possible because the students are freed of the burden of guessing at words in reading. Their attention targets something larger: comprehension of content.

The Foundation's approach encourages teachers to read aloud to children at the end of a lesson at a higher level than the children can read by themselves. Teachers can read Greek myths, fairy tales, adventure stories, and histories to them. Even reading to the students for five minutes can be valuable. This strategy encourages the students to work and become even more proficient readers. The material increases their vocabulary, widens their knowledge and exposes them to more elevated language.

The pace of learning accelerates. By the second and third grade, students trained in this method are given literature as their textbooks. The children are encouraged to write and contribute to the dialogue of ideas. They are given the tools to write poems, plays, stories and essays. They must be given knowledge about which to write: hence the emphasis on Greek myths, history and science as reading material.

Composition

After the students in first grade have written and analyzed thirty or forty words in their notebooks, they can begin to write simple sentences using those words. The teacher has modeled sentences orally all along by putting vocabulary words into sentences before writing them and dictating them. Now the teacher has to explain that all sentences begin with a capital letter and end with a period or a question mark. The students have to say sentences and then write them. They have to learn that all sentences have a subject and a verb or action word for the subject to do. Then after practice-writing one sentence, they can try to write another sentence related to the first sentence, and so on.

If the children have been listening to Greek myths, *Robin Hood*, stories about knights in armor, or biographies and history, they have subjects to write about that are far more interesting than compositions on, "What I Did Over the Summer." Knowledge of a wider world can also stimulate fictional stories. This allows students to learn the difference between story writing, or fiction, and factual informative writing.

The current practice of having students write freely without regard to proper spelling, called "invented spelling," is destructive, because it imprints the wrong spelling on the brain. Writing carefully from the beginning reinforces correct spelling and usage and actually gives students the tools to write with far greater ease. It permits the children to read back accurately what they have written.

Good sentence construction and grammar can be taught as the students progress through the grades. This kind of instruction will prepare the students for the middle grades and junior high school because it will build up from simple book reports to more complicated research papers.

The great lack of writing skills is evident in colleges being forced to teach writing, as well as law firms and corporations being forced to teach writing to college graduates. High school students should have the opportunity to write well-researched papers on a topic of interest to them with footnotes and bibliography. One lone pioneer, Will Fitzhugh, who started the *Concord Review* to which students submit their research papers, has espoused this need for years. (see appendix)

Taking pleasure in composing stories, essays, and letters all begins in first grade. The ability to organize and compose one's thoughts encourages the "critical thinking" that is so much discussed in educational literature. This is developed with first, an analysis of words, and then with setting one's ideas down in an organized way.

> *"I would rather stop breathing*
> than to give up teaching this way."
> AMY HILL, *teacher, P.S. 282, Brooklyn*

Reading Reform teacher trainers gather for their monthly meeting.

CHAPTER VI

Comments of Principals, Teachers, Students and Mentors

THE READING REFORM FOUNDATION IN-SCHOOL TEACHER-Training Program earns devotion from principals, teachers, consultants and parents because it works.

Principals who have worked with the program are quick to point out that the benefits extend to a broad population. Olga Iris Guzman, the principal of P.S. 228 in Queens writes, "Phonics was the ingredient that was missing and which Reading Reform provides in its training. Children can come from any neighborhood and still learn." Principal Kenneth Thomas of C.S. 134 in the Bronx laments the time that testing takes away from learning. When asked his vision of what this school should provide, he declares, "When students leave here, they should be able to pick up a newspaper and use their minds for critical thinking. You can't teach kindergarten, or grades 1, 2, and 3 here unless you are trained by Reading Reform Foundation."

At any given school, one class might be using the program while the class of the same grade is not. Charlotte Haber, supervisor of the Reading Reform Foundation Spalding program, another Orton method and long-time Reading Reform Foundation mentor says, "I was working in a slower kindergarten than another kindergarten right next door. At half-term, when the other teacher was absent, many children from her class were sent in to sit with our class. My kids had their own little books, were opening them, and were busy reading. The children from the other class did not want the books because they did not have the skills to read. The children we worked with couldn't wait to get the books and try out the words."

Two students from P.S. 28 in the Bronx stopped one of the Reading Reform Foundation consultants in the hall to report that they had won prizes for being the top readers in the third grade. One of them said, "Thank you for teaching us to read." Another child who had difficulty learning to read wrote, "I love learning to read with Reading Reform and now I want to read and read."

Students are not the only beneficiaries of the program. Judy Muniz, who has been with Reading Reform Foundation for 14 years, notes that teachers often approach her to say that teaching the program has made them better spellers. Judy continues, "They said, 'I can read, but I didn't know there were rules that govern thousands of words.'"

Donna Moffet, a teacher of first grade at P.S. 161 in Manhattan, notes how the program's value extends beyond reading alone. "Throughout the day, throughout the curriculum, my first-graders excitedly make connections back to our early morning Reading Reform lessons. During independent reading time, one may say, 'Ms. M. Look! I found –er, hammer –er!' while another approaches, showing me a book, and points out, 'Wow! We just learned this: boot, -oo!'" During a read-aloud, another child, recalling suffixes, notes the __ing and __ed endings. I'm impressed with their six-year-old memories as well as the integration and synthesis of their learning."

Margaret Padua teaches third grade at P.S. 152 in Manhattan. She wrote about her experience teaching *The Odyssey*, "I have enjoyed all aspects of Reading Reform, yet nothing in my teaching has ever come close to reading *The Odyssey* with this class. The students and I are learning wonderful content, have amazing conversations,

DRAWING BY THIRD-GRADE STUDENT

Cyclops from The Odyssey

LETTER

Third-grader. P.S. 152

Dear Mrs Rose,

Thank you for letting us Read The Odyssey all Together as a class.

Odysseus had alot of adventures so far. In the beginning, The suitors wanted to marry Queen Penelope. Queen Penelope is Odysseuss wife. The suitors Thought Odysseus was dead. Then, Odysseus has been away from home. Odysseus didn't see his son. Odysseus misses his island Ithca. After that, he starts for home. but he lands on the cyclops's Island. The Cyclops is son of persidon. odysseus blinded the cyclops. another Event was; the land of the dead. The river Styx in the land of the dead. it is cold in the land of the dead

sincerely,
Rachel

P.S. My favorite part was when Odysseus blinded the cyclops. It was scary and Funny all at the same Time. Thank you so much for the book It is amazing.

and are enjoying ourselves tremendously with the text. One student's comment is particularly memorable to me. We were working on our letters to you when I reminded the students to make sure they expressed their thanks to Mrs. Rose for sending us *The Odyssey*. A student raised his hand and asked, 'Why are we thanking Mrs. Rose? Didn't Homer write *The Odyssey?*'"

A teacher at P.S. 282 in Brooklyn, Amy Hill, notes, "The parents are so excited by the program. One parent sat in on a lesson just to see how well her child was doing. She couldn't believe what she witnessed and how well he was reading."

Some students face unusual challenges, and Reading Reform has contributed to their ability to get up to speed in reading. Helen Hamblin writes about one student in her first-grade class at P.S. 28 in Manhattan: "M. spoke only Arabic so no one was able to communicate with him. He would walk around the room, scribble on any paper given to him and then rip up the paper. At some point, M. made a complete turnaround. He now sits still, takes part in class work and attempts to do the work. M. told me that he now wants to pay attention and learn, and he has been doing just that."

Here are three additional reports from teachers. The first is from Ana Bravo, a third-grade teacher at P.S. 152 in Manhattan who was new to Reading Reform: "You know, I have been teaching for over 20 years. What have I been doing up until now?" Amy Leopold-Esposito, a kindergarten teacher at P.S. 138 in the Bronx, writes, "I was so happy to hear my students tell me they read *Tim* (a book) all by themselves for homework. My first-graders had such confidence that it brought tears to my eyes because my class is considered low-functioning readers. Reading Reform is helping my students become confident readers and writers...and it is only October! I can see their progression every day."

Consultants love hearing feedback from students and their parents, especially when they describe how the children have internalized the lessons and mastered the principles of reading. Finally, Bonnie Lee

Apple, training at the Parker Elementary School in Mount Vernon, New York, describes a conversation she had with a reading teacher who has 25 years of experience: "She told me I saved her life this year. Reading Reform Foundation training is the missing link she has been looking for her whole career."

LETTER

Community School 150
920 East 157th Street
Bronx, NY 10459
Tel: (718) 328-7729

Edwin Irizarry, Principal
Renzo Martinez, Assistant Principal
Norma Sanchez, Assistant Principal
Fax: (718) 589-7590

May 11, 20011

Re: Reading Reform

Dear Sir/Madam:

We have had the Reading Reform program for 7 years. All of our Kindergarten –3rd grade teachers have been trained in this phonics-based program by a cadre of dedicated reading experts.

I can state with conviction that this program has assisted our lower grade children to excel in their reading tasks. Our classroom teachers rave about the merits of the program when I visit their classrooms.

The evidence has been in the growth of the children as they transition from the lower grades to the upper grades.

I strongly recommend the Reading Reform program to every principal. They will see immediate results.

Please feel free to contact me at 718-328-7729 if you require additional information.

Professionally,

Edwin Irizarry
Principal

DRAWING

Child's rendition of The Odyssey.

Writing about what one has read is important, too.

CHAPTER VII

Testing and Analysis of the Results

2010–2011

ALTHOUGH THE EMPHASIS OF THE WORK OF READING REFORM Foundation is on the training of regular classroom teachers, one cannot discuss a good teacher-training program without including the results of testing the children involved. Students were tested at the beginning and the end of the school year.

Dr. Linnea Ehri, Distinguished Professor, Program in Educational Psychology of the Graduate Center of the City University of New York, supervised the analysis of all scores sent to her in a blind form. The names of the children, classroom teachers and Reading Reform Foundation trainers were sent to her, coded by letter and number.

These variables were considered in the analysis:

ESL (English as a Second Language) or bilingual students
Students identified with ADD (attention deficit disorder) speech
   or hearing impairment, autism
Students who had been in a Reading Reform Foundation
   program previously

The age, experience and gender of the classroom teacher
Number of students in the class

It must be stated at the outset the teachers Reading Reform Foundation was working with were diligent, enthusiastic and hardworking. Teachers were dealing with a variety of children's abilities and problems that are not dealt with in most charter schools and private schools. For example, the percentage of children who were in ESL or bilingual classes is indicated below:

Kindergarten – out of 530 students,
    30% were in bilingual or ESL classes
First grade – out of 406 students,
    30% were in bilingual or ESL classes
Second grade – out of 325 students,
    19% were in bilingual or ESL classes

The percentage of children with a wide range of learning problems is as below:

Kindergarten – 12%
First grade – 12%
Second grade – 11%

A great deal of credit must be given to the classroom teachers who deal with these challenges day after day.

What follows is an excerpted word summary of the analysis, developed by Dr. Ehri and Dr. Bert Flugman, of testing, as well as figures and tables included in their report.

Method

PARTICIPANTS. Teachers from kindergarten through third grade completed the year-long program: 26 kindergarten teachers, 21 first grade teachers, 16 second grade teachers, and four third grade teachers. All but six of the 67 teachers were female. The mean age was 41 years. The mean number of previous years of teaching experience was 11.8 and ranged from 1 to 36 years. There were 40 teachers who received Orton Gillingham-based and 27 who received Spalding instruction. The types of classrooms were varied and included the following: 44 general education classes, 8 bilingual/ESL classes, 2 dual language classes, 7 collaborative team teaching classes, 4 inclusion classes, and 2 combination classes. Class sizes ranged from 11 to 30 students, with a mean of 22 students across classes.

A total of 1,336 students completed the school year in these teachers' classrooms and were assessed on at least one pretest and one posttest. There were 530 kindergartners, 406 first graders, 325 second graders, and 75 third graders.

ACHIEVEMENT TESTS. Tests were given to measure students' letter-sound knowledge, reading and spelling abilities. The tests were administered in the fall as pretests and in the spring as posttests. The following tests were given at each grade level:

1. Kindergarten
   Measure of letter and letter-sound knowledge: Sands (15 items);
      Gates-MacGinitie subtest (30 items)
   Measure of spelling: Sands (5 words); Morrison-McCall
      (10 words) (posttest only)
2. First Grade
   Measure of letter-sound knowledge: Sands (18 items)
      (pretest only)

Measure of word decoding: Gates-MacGinitie subtest
(43 items)

Measure of spelling: Sands (10 words) (pretest only); Morrison-McCall (15 words on pretest; 30 words on posttest)

3. Second Grade

Measure of word decoding: Gates-MacGinitie subtest
(43 items)

Measure of reading comprehension: Gates-MacGinitie subtest
(39 items)

Measure of spelling: Morrison-McCall (30 words)

4. Third Grade

Measure of reading comprehension: Gates-MacGinitie subtest
(48 items)

Measure of spelling: Morrison-McCall (40 words)

The study did not include comparison classrooms whose teachers did not receive RRF professional development, so no information could be provided about the gains that would have occurred among teachers and students who did not participate in the RRF program. In the absence of this data, attempts were made to provide other types of information about expected levels of performance and the size of the gains from fall to spring. This included using information provided in the Gates-MacGinitie and Morrison-McCall test manuals to convert mean performance to grade-equivalent (GE) scores. It included comparing mean performance of RRF students to the fall and spring mean scores of the representative sample of students used to create norms for the Gates-MacGinitie subtests. Finally, Cohen's *d* effect size statistic was calculated to indicate the extent of growth from the beginning to the end of the year on tests that were given in the fall and repeated in the spring. It is calculated by subtracting the mean on the pretest from the mean on the posttest and dividing by the *SD*. An effect size of 1.00 indicates that the difference between means was one standard deviation. According to Cohen's (1988) rule of thumb, a value of 0.20 indicates a small effect, 0.50 a moderate effect, and 0.80 or greater a large effect.

Results

KINDERGARTEN. In kindergarten, students' knowledge of letters and letter-sound relations and their ability to spell words were pretested in the fall and post-tested in the spring. The first question of interest was how much students improved over the year. Their average performance on the various tests was examined. Results are reported in Table 1. On the Sands letter-sound posttest at the end of the year, the mean was close to perfect (i.e., 14.7 correct out of 15 maximum). In fact, 87% of the kindergartners had perfect scores. On the Gates letters and letter-sound posttest, the average score on the posttest was very high as well. In fact, 80% of the kindergartners were correct on at least 80% of the test items, regarded by some as indicating a mastery level of performance.

Growth in letter-sound knowledge from September to May was substantial. This was indicated by the effect size statistic, Cohen's *d*, reported in Table 1. On all three tests, the effect size was large or very large, ranging from 1.15 to 2.24. This indicates impressive growth from fall to spring.

Novice beginning readers are known to have great difficulty spelling words correctly before they have received formal instruction in reading. This is because they have weak or non-existent knowledge of letter-sound relations and little practice reading or writing words. As evident in Table 1, at the beginning of kindergarten, 82% of the children were unable to spell any words correctly on the Sands spelling pretest. However, during the year their spelling ability improved, and by the end of the year, only 8% of the students were still at this low level. On the spelling posttests, children spelled a mean of 74% of the words correctly on the Sands, and they spelled a mean of 54% of the words correctly on the Morrison-McCall test. Norms on the MM test placed kindergartners at an average grade equivalent level of 1.9. However, this test was published over 50 years ago, so the validity of its norms remains uncertain. Even so, the year-end mean spelling score of these kindergartners was impressive.

From Figures 1 and 2, it is evident that classrooms of kindergartners began the school year at very different levels, with some classes knowing few and others knowing most letter-sounds on average. This meant that some teachers had much more work to do than others. However, by the end of the year, most had achieved success. Regardless of how poorly students performed in the fall, by the spring most of the classrooms showed very high average levels of performance. Classrooms with the lowest fall scores showed very large gains, and by the end of the year their average scores were at the same level as classes who began the year with much higher scores. Impressively, on the Sands letter-sound test, most of the class means were close to perfect. These findings show that most teachers were effective in teaching letters and letter-sounds to their kindergartners. It is likely that the professional development and instructional guidance provided by the RRF consultants contributed strongly to their success.

FIRST GRADE. Students were given two tests in both the fall and spring to assess growth in their reading and spelling ability during the year. Mean performance is shown in Table 2. In decoding words, first graders began the year by performing at a level expected of first graders in the fall shown by a grade equivalent level of 1.1 based on Gates-MacGinitie test norms. By the end of the year they were performing at the level expected in the spring, with a mean grade equivalent of 1.9. Calculation of Cohen's d revealed that the effect size from fall to spring was very large, 1.69. Comparison of first graders' posttest mean to that of students in the Gates norming sample showed that the RRF students outperformed the norming sample by a grade equivalent level of two months (see Table 2). These findings indicate that the RRF program was very effective in teaching first graders to decode words.

Students were given the Morrison-McCall spelling test in the fall and spring. From mean scores in Table 2, it is evident that first graders' ability to spell words correctly rose by almost one grade equivalent level, from 1.9 to 2.8. The growth from fall to spring showed a very large effect size of 1.70. These results suggest that the RRF program was most effective in teaching first graders to spell words.

SECOND GRADE. The reading achievement of second graders was assessed in the fall and spring with three tests: the word decoding subtest and the reading comprehension subtest of the Gates, and the Morrison-McCall word spelling test. Mean performance of the sample of second graders is reported in Table 3. Raw scores were transformed into grade equivalent (GE) levels based on norms provided in the test manuals.

It is apparent from Table 3 that on the word decoding test given in the fall, second graders were performing somewhat below the level expected for second grade, with a grade equivalent mean of 1.8. This was not unexpected, given that the students came from urban public schools having many low income and minority students known to perform below expected levels in reading. By the end of the year, students' mean performance had improved to a grade equivalent level of 2.3. The substantial growth in decoding words was indicated by a large effect size of 1.05. Comparison of RRF students to the Gates-MacGinitie norming sample of students revealed superior growth from fall to spring for the RRF second graders. In the fall, the RRF students performed below the norming sample (i.e., 1.8 vs. 2.1 GE) but by the end of the year, the RRF students had almost caught up to the norming sample (i.e., 2.3 vs. 2.4 GE). The effect size from fall to spring of the norming sample was moderate and only half that of the RRF effect size which was large (i.e., 0.48 vs. 1.05, as shown in Table 3). These findings reveal that the growth in word decoding skill achieved by second graders taught by RRF teachers was substantial and greater than that expected.

Second graders also improved in their reading comprehension. As evident in Table 3, the mean score was below grade level in the fall, with GE = 1.7. However, by the spring the mean score had improved to a grade equivalent level of 2.2. The large effect size of 1.01 indicates that this gain is impressive. This is further supported by a comparison of the RRF students to the norming sample whose growth was only half this great, showing a moderate effect size of only 0.47 (see Table 3). Whereas the RRF students began second grade with a GE score that was much lower than that of the norming sample (i.e., RRF GE of 1.7 vs. norming sample of 2.1), by the end of second grade, the two GE levels were more similar (i.e., RRF GE of 2.2 vs. norming sample of 2.4). This is further evidence that the growth in second graders' reading comprehension promoted by RRF instruction was greater than expected even though RRF students' performance was still below the expected level.

Improvement in second graders' spelling ability was impressive. Mean performance on the Morrison-McCall spelling test in the fall in Table 3 shows that second graders were spelling words at a second grade equivalent level. By the end of the year their performance had increase a full grade equivalent level, according to test norms. The effect size was large, showing that substantial growth occurred from fall to spring.

In sum, these findings indicate that the RRF program was effective in promoting substantial growth in second grade students' ability to decode and spell words and to comprehend text. Most second grade teachers were very effective in providing instruction to support this growth.

THIRD GRADE. Fewer third grade teachers and students participated in the RRF program than in the lower grades. There were four teachers and 75 third graders. Students were given the Gates reading comprehension test and the MM spelling test at the beginning and end of the year. Mean performance is shown in Table 4.

As evident in Table 4, students entered third grade with a mean reading comprehension score placing them at a low second GE level (GE = 2.3). By the end of the year, the mean had been raised to a GE of 3.1. The effect size indicating the extent of growth from fall to spring was 0.87, which is large. In fact, it was three times as large as the growth achieved by the norming sample, showing a small/moderate effect size of 0.31. Nevertheless, the RRF sample performed only at a 3.1 GE level at the end of the year, substantially below that of the norming sample performing at a 3.5 GE level. This indicates that, according to test norms, the RRF students on average were a year behind their expected reading comprehension level at the end of third grade. Although disappointing, this is perhaps not surprisingly given the fact that the RRF students were enrolled in inner city, urban schools serving populations of low income, minority children.

These findings are consistent with results of other studies indicating that low income, minority students fall increasingly behind peers from middle class schools as they proceed through the grades. The RRF program very likely contributes by mitigating the decline, particularly through its instruction in word reading and spelling. It may be less effective in strengthening students' ability to read and comprehend text because this ability requires not only on effective decoding skill but also knowledge sources that are harder to raise to grade equivalent levels through instruction, principally vocabulary and background knowledge in a wide variety of content areas.

Summary of Study

Findings of the present study show that teachers who received RRF instruction and guidance from consultants were very effective in improving the reading and spelling achievement of their students. Their effectiveness was evident in all of the grades, from kindergarten through third grade. Growth was substantial on all of the measures. Even though students and classrooms may have entered grades performing below expected levels, the growth that they exhibited during the school year was impressive. This was indicated by the effect size statistic assessing the extent of improvement from the beginning to the end of the year in standardized units, with 0.80 considered large. Effect sizes across all of the measures and grades were large and some were very large. Values ranged from 0.87 among third graders to 2.24 among kindergartners.

All of the teachers were effective in raising achievement levels substantially on at least some of the measures. Kindergarten teachers increased their students' average letter-sound knowledge to near perfect levels, indicating mastery. Those teaching students with weaker knowledge at the start of school produced the greatest growth so that by the end of the year their students were performing at the same level as the other classes that were initially more advanced.

First grade teachers were uniformly successful in teaching word decoding and spelling. The extent of growth shown by their students from fall to spring was impressive. The majority of classes met if not exceed grade level expectations on the word decoding and spelling tests by the end of the year.

Much more variability was evident across the classes of second grade teachers. The word decoding, reading comprehension and spelling skills of some classes in the fall were very low while other classes performed at higher entry levels. The amount of growth from fall to spring was also variable among teachers. However, most of the classes showed greater growth than that shown by the Gates norming sample. Effect sizes reflecting the extent of growth were large.

The third grade teachers produced large and consistent gains in their students' spelling performance from fall to spring. Reading comprehension gains were more variable across classes. However, growth in most of the classes was greater than that of the Gates-MacGinitie norming sample.

References for CUNY Testing Study

Brady, S. (2011). Efficacy of phonics teaching for reading outcomes: Indications from post-NRP research. In S. Brady, D. Braze, & C. Fowler (Eds.), *Explaining individual differences in reading: Theory and evidence* (pp. 69-96). New York: Psychology Press.

Cohen, J. (1988). *Statistical power analysis for the behavior sciences* (2nd ed.). Hillsdale, NJ: Erlbaum.

Maria, K., & Hughes, K. (2008). *Gates-MacGinitie reading tests: Technical report supplement*. Rolling Meadows, IL: Riverside.

Moats, L. (1994). Knowledge of language: The missing foundation for teacher education. *Annals of Dyslexia, 44,* 81-102.

National Reading Panel (2000). *Teaching Children to Read: An Evidence-Based Assessment of the Scientific Research Literature on Reading and Its Implications for Reading Instruction: Report of the Subgroups.* National Institute of Child Health and Human Development, and the National Instititue for Literacy.

Slavin, R., Lake, C., Chambers, B., Cheung, A. & Davis, S. (2009). Effective reading programs for the elementary grades: A best-evidence synthesis. *Review of Educational Research, 79,* 1391-1466.

TABLE I

Mean performance of Kindergarteners on Pretests and Posttests

Test	Pretest		Posttest		Effect Size
	M	SD	M	SD	d^a
ALL STUDENTS					
Sands Letter-Sounds (15 max)	8.49	(5.4)	14.70	(1.2)	1.15
% scores of zero	13%		0.2%		
% scores of 100%	15%		87%		
Gates Letters & Sounds (30 max)	14.25	(7.6)	25.92	(4.2)	1.98
% scores ≥ 80%	13%		80%		
Sands Spelling Words (5 max)	0.35	(.85)	3.94	(1.6)	2.24
% scores of zero	82%		8%		
MM Spelling Words (10 max)	—	—	5.46	(3.0)	
Grade-equivalent			1.9		

Note. There were 530 kindergartners in the total sample. Due to missing data, the number of observations per mean ranged from N = 494 to 527.

[a] Effects sizes indicate the standardized mean gain from fall to spring. The statistic is Cohen's d calculated by subtracting the pretest mean from the posttest mean and dividing by the pooled SD. If the size of a SD at one test point was reduced by floor or ceiling effects, then only the larger SD was used in the calculation. According to Cohen's (1988) rule of thumb, 0.20 are small effects, 0.50 moderate effects, and 0.80 or greater are large.

TABLE 2

Mean Performance of First Graders on Pretests and Posttests

Test	Pretest		Posttest		Effect Size[a]
	M	*SD*	*M*	*SD*	*d*
ALL STUDENTS					
Sands Letter-Sounds (18 max)	15.42	(3.8)	—	—	
Sands Letter-Sounds (10 max)	5.63	(3.3)	—	—	
Gates Word Decoding (43 max)	16.62	(8.9)	31.47	(8.7)	1.69
Grade-equivalent	1.1		1.9		
Norming Sample[b]	—		27.76	(10.1)	
Grade-equivalent			1.7		
MM Spelling Words	16.62	(8.9)	31.47	(8.7)	1.69
Pretest (15 words)	4.79	(3.5)			
Grade-equivalent	1.9				
Posttest (30 words)			13.80	(5.3)	1.70
Grade-equivalent			2.8		

Note. There were 406 first graders in the total sample. Due to missing data, the number of observations per mean ranged from $N = 386$ to 403.

[a] Effects sizes indicate the standardized mean gain from fall to spring. The statistic is Cohen's *d* calculated by subtracting the pretest mean from the posttest mean and dividing by the pooled SD. According to Cohen's (1988) rule of thumb, 0.20 are small effects, 0.50 moderate effects, and 0.80 or greater are large.
[b] The norming sample means were drawn from the Gates MacGinitie Technical Report Supplement (Maria & Hughes, 2008). These show the performance of the representative sample

TABLE 3

Mean Performance of Second Graders on Pretests and Posttests

Test	Pretest		Posttest		Effect Size[a]
	M	SD	M	SD	d
ALL STUDENTS					
Gates Word Decoding (43 max)	23.05	(10.6)	33.22	(8.8)	1.05
Grade-equivalent	1.8		2.3		
Norming Sample[b]	29.45	(9.8)	33.78	(8.5)	0.48
Grade-equivalent	2.1		2.4		
Gates Reading Compreh. (39 max)	19.88	(8.4)	27.80	(7.3)	1.01
Grade-equivalent	1.7		2.2		
Norming Sample[b]	26.79	(8.4)	30.43	(7.1)	0.47
Grade-equivalent	2.1		2.4		
MM Word Spelling (30 max)	12.61	(6.2)	18.97	(6.5)	1.00
Grade-equivalent	2.7		3.7		

Note. There were 325 second graders in the total sample. Due to missing data, the number of observations per mean ranged from N = 309 to 321.

[a] Effects sizes indicate the standardized mean gain from fall to spring. The statistic is Cohen's d calculated by subtracting the pretest mean from the posttest mean and dividing by the pooled SD. According to Cohen's (1988) rule of thumb, 0.20 are small effects, 0.50 moderate effects, and 0.80 or greater are large.

[b] The norming sample means were drawn from the Gates MacGinitie Technical Report Supplement (Maria & Hughes, 2008). These show the performance of the representative sample of second graders tested in the fall and spring for the purpose of creating norms for scores on the test.

TABLE 4

Mean Performance of Third Graders on Pretests and Posttests

Test	Pretest		Posttest		Effect Size
	M	*SD*	*M*	*SD*	*d*[a]
ALL STUDENTS					
Gates Reading Comprehension (48 max)	18.27	(7.7)	25.67	(9.3)	0.87
Grade-equivalent	2.3		3.1		
Norming Sample	27.85	(10.7)	31.11	(10.1)	0.31
Grade-equivalent	3.2		3.5		
MM Word Spelling (30 max)	19.99	(6.1)	25.28	(5.8)	0.89
Grade-equivalent	3.9		4.7		

Note. There were 75 third graders in the total sample. Due to missing data, the number of observations per mean ranged from $N = 73$ to 75.

[a] Effects sizes indicate the standardized mean gain from fall to spring. The statistic is Cohen's *d* calculated by subtracting the pretest mean from the posttest mean and dividing by the pooled *SD*. According to Cohen's (1988) rule of thumb, 0.20 are small effects, 0.50 moderate effects, and 0.80 or greater are large.

[b] The norming sample means were drawn from the Gates MacGinitie Technical Report Supplement (Maria & Hughes, 2008). These show the performance of the representative sample of third graders tested in the fall and spring for the purpose of creating norms for scores on the test.

FIGURE 1

Mean improvement from Fall to Spring on Sands Letter Sound Test Across All Classrooms (M), and for Classrooms of Individual Kindergarten Teachers (T) (Maximum correct=15)

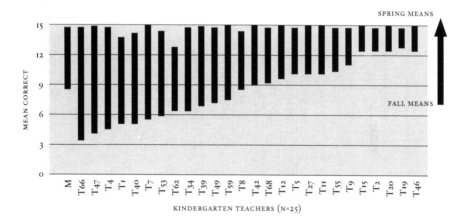

FIGURE 2

Mean Improvement from Fall to Spring on Gates (Level PR) Letters and Letter sound Subtest Across All Classrooms (M), and for Classrooms of Individual Kindergarten Teachers (T) (Maximum correct=30)

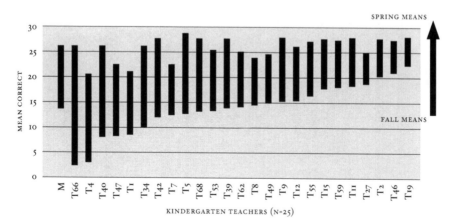

FIGURE 3

Mean Improvement from Fall to Spring on Gates Decoding Subtest Across All Classrooms (M), and for Classrooms of Individual First Grade Teachers (T) (Maximum correct=43)

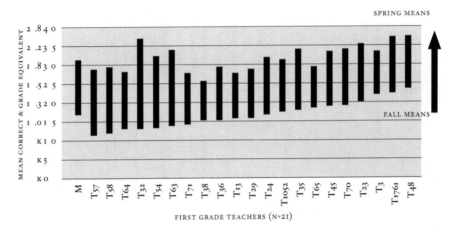

FIGURE 4

Mean Improvement from Fall to Spring on Morrison MacCall Spelling Test Across All Classrooms (M), and for Classrooms of Individual First Grade Teachers (T) (Max correct=15 for Fall; Max correct=30 for Spring)

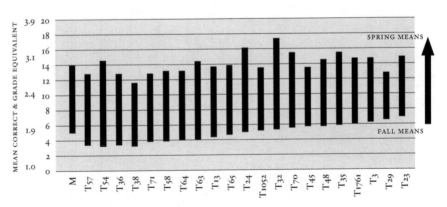

FIGURE 5

Mean Improvement from Fall to Spring on
Gates Word Decoding Subtest for Norming Sample (N),
Across All Classrooms (M), and for Classrooms for Individual
Second Grade Teachers (T) (Maximum correct=43)

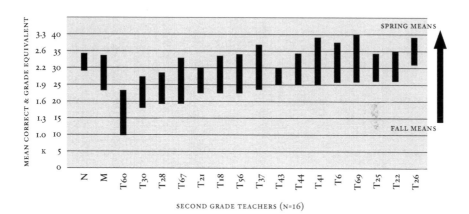

FIGURE 6

Mean Improvement from Fall to Spring on
Gates Reading Comprehension Subtest for Norming Sample (N),
Across All Classrooms (M), and for Classrooms of Individual
Second Grade Teachers (T) (Maximum correct=39)

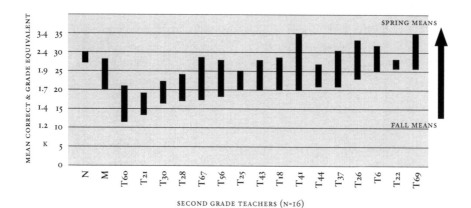

FIGURE 7

Mean Improvement from Fall to Spring on Morrison MacCall Spelling Test Across All Classrooms (M), and for Classrooms of Individual Second Grade Teachers (T) (Maximum correct=30)

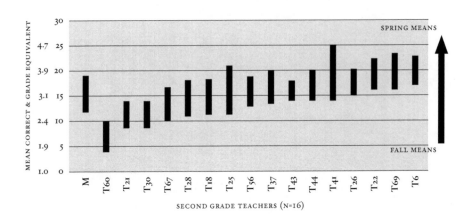

FIGURE 8

Mean Improvement from Fall to Spring for Norming Sample (N), for Total Classrooms (M), and for Classrooms of Individual Third Grade Teachers (T)

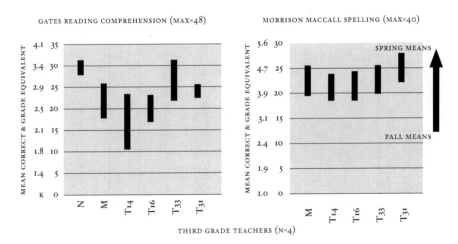

"You're the ones that save children.
Your program should be required in every classroom."
CELIA KAPLINSKY, Principal, P.S. 216, Brooklyn

CHAPTER VIII

Conclusions

SAVING AMERICAN EDUCATION: ONE TEACHER & 30 CHILDREN AT A TIME

THE 30-YEAR EXPERIENCE OF READING REFORM FOUNDATION has shown that these factors are essential to a successful classroom teacher-training program in the teaching of reading, writing, spelling and comprehension:

Precise and substantive training of the *mentors* to the classroom teachers in a 40-45 hour multisensory phonics course as well as a school year of shadowing and working with an experienced mentor-consultant.

Precise and substantive training in a 40-45 hour multisensory phonics course for the classroom teachers.

Close cooperation with administrators and principals so that they understand the requirements in time and goals of the training program and participate wholeheartedly.

Following the course training for the classroom teachers with twice-a-week visits by trained consultants for two one-hour preparation periods and two one-hour classroom working visits per week, for a total of 60 visits per year (120 hours). The preparation period is used to plan the week's lessons, to discuss problems and to practice techniques. The classroom visits allow for the consultant to demonstrate how the multi-sensory phonics instruction is delivered to the children, with the classroom teacher gradually taking over as the year progresses. At the end of the year the result is a well-trained classroom teacher capable of using this approach in all the future years of his or her teaching career.

The excellent supervision provided by Reading Reform Foundation. This takes many forms: monthly visits; encouragement of nightly telephone calls from the Reading Reform consultants to the director of the in-school program to iron out immediate problems; monthly, brief reports from the consultants that alert supervisors to successes and problems.

Monthly three-hour luncheon meetings of the consultants at the main office where teaching techniques and problems can be discussed, and demonstrations of good teaching can be given. Testing materials and books and supplies for the students are distributed at this time.

Emphasis on friendly demeanor and desire to help. Reading Reform Foundation supervisors and trainers understand that they are guests in the schools and that they are there to be pleasant to everyone, and patient and collegial with the classroom teachers with whom they are working.

Reading Reform Foundation has to raise 80% of the program costs, with only 20% charged to the public schools.

The total cost of the training and the materials is $12,500.00 per classroom per year. The $2,500 fee can be borne by a school district because the investment is in the future years of a teacher's professional life.

Bottom-up implementation. Reading Reform instinctively feels that training two to four classroom teachers in a school the first year is more effective than a blanket fiat over a whole school. This way, when these few classroom teachers tell others in their school of the successes of their students in learning, the other teachers willingly ask to be trained and often, in subsequent years, all the early kindergarten through second-grade teachers are included.

In addition to all the anecdotal evidence of the students' improvement, over the years the noticeable improvement in reading scores has convinced principals and teachers of the efficacy of this program.

This efficient, thorough, substantive kind of training needs to be given in every school district in the United States. Privileged children as well as unprivileged children need the explanation of the English language that this provides. The intellectual yet practical approach to teaching, reading, writing, spelling and comprehension can be copied and implemented everywhere. It requires hard work on the part of the mentor-consultants, on the part of the supervisors and on the part of the classroom teachers. It even needs hard work on the part of the students. The early and continuous successes as the program proceeds in the year engages them all.

LETTER

Class 2-301
6/4/10

Dear Ms Nathanson,

Ms. Nathanson you know lots of things. you taught our teacher lots of things and now Ms. M is teaching us the same things. Ms Nathanson you can read big words and you teach them to us that is how we lean because you teach us those words. thank you for the things you gave us.

Sincerely, Lorraine

me   Ms Nathanson

LETTER

class 203

May 18, 2009

I am writing to thank you for
the book that you gave to me.
I would Like to thank you because
I Like the pictures in the book
I want to read to my sister.
I love all the stories in the book
I love the characters in the story.
I can think about is happening in the
story. It is really amazing.

Thank you
Joanna

Emotional Health

One component of the program is the emotional health of the teacher and his or her students in a Reading Reform classroom. This has not been measured, but a visit to any one of the classrooms reveals a high degree of engagement on the part of the students and a sense of successful teaching on the part of the teacher. This sense of mutual accomplishment feeds on itself, creating a palpable excitement evident to any visitor.

The teacher gets constant feedback because of the structure of the lessons. He or she can observe each morning which child is holding back a bit or having difficulty. Similarly, the children can see how they are doing each day in the spelling, vocabulary and reading lessons. In each instance where children have made a mistake, there is an opportunity to correct their own work.

Students who have difficulty sitting still or focusing on the subject at hand often are calmed by the regular routine of the lessons. They know what to expect and what is expected of them.

Teachers new to this kind of training are amazed at how much the students can absorb. The students, on the other hand, push their teachers for more in their excitement with the power of language and of their learning.

Success breeds success for the teacher and the students. These are happy classrooms.

CHAPTER IX

Closing Thoughts

THE ESSENTIAL KEYS TO THE WHOLE SUCCESS OF THE READING Reform Foundation program are the phonetic, multisensory instruction in the beginning teaching of reading, writing, and spelling and the sustained, twice-weekly mentoring of the classroom teachers. This intensive year-long training provides high quality professional development for teachers that is missing currently in American teacher preparation.

But there is one other element that cannot be emphasized enough. As the teacher and the children write vocabulary words, they analyze them as to sounds, appropriate spelling rules, syllabication and meaning. Hence the title of this book. First-grade students should not write 'Sun day' mindlessly. They delight in figuring out that it is named for the sun. Often guided by the teacher, they leap to the conclusion that 'Mon day' is named for the moon. This is the beginning of comprehension.

This careful analysis of words, often as new to the teacher as to the students, is the beginning of the intellectual journey that is the birthright of every child. Let us train teachers to clarify their understanding of English so that they can transmit a rational system to their students.

We must open children to the distinctions of sound and meaning between 'house' and 'home', 'love' and 'leave', 'thank' and 'think', 'lawful' and 'lawless', 'cheat' and 'check'. We must permit them to hone their minds on fine differences. We must respect young people enough to encourage them to think and write precisely.

We cannot deny the soaring beauty of words, the exquisite shades of meanings, and the playfulness of puns that delight all children. They must carry on, use, and shape the incredible tool that is language – so logical in its development, so precise in its countless nuances of meanings, not even comprehended by computers. It is at once mind-forming and formed by fertile minds. This heritage, this great English language, rich with all the languages that have flowed into it, replete with history, bursts with vitality and new creation.

Can the mastery of language in all its precision and infinite variety be denied to children of the inner-city and children of affluent suburbs? Understanding the distinctions between the author's choice of words is where comprehension of written material begins. This provides the firm basis on which all study in higher grades, junior high, high school and college can build.

Our job, as teachers, in first grade and always, is to teach the child to begin those careful acts of discernment in reading that train the child, grown adult, to make distinctions between shoddy and worthy ideas, flimsy and sturdy values, enduring and fleeting emotions.

This, then, is the path that education in these glorious United States must take.

Acknowledgements

These people influenced Reading Reform Foundation's thinking in profound ways:

Isaac Asimov
Miriam Balmuth
Jacques Barzun
Jeanne S. Chall
Rudolf Flesch
Emily Goldberg
Sylvia Goldsmith
Diane Ravitch
Romalda Bishop Spalding
Leona D. Spector
Charles C. Walcutt

These people labored to make Reading Reform Foundation of New York strong, effective and influential:

Louise L. Arias
Aileen Lewisohn Godsick
Lauren Wedeles
Margaret Whelan

These loyal Board of Trustees members have provided their sage advice and material generosity over many years:

Louise L. Arias, President
Aileen Lewisohn Godsick, Vice-President
Leona D. Spector, Vice-President
Judith Frost Levine, Secretary
Sandra Priest Rose, Chairman & Treasurer
Lauren Wedeles, Executive Director

Ronnie Eldridge, former City Council Member
Daniel Garodnick, City Council Member
Robert Jackson, City Council Member
Joel Rivera, City Council Member
Ydanis Rodriguez, City Council Member
Scott Stringer, President of the Borough of Manhattan
The New York City Department of Education
The New York City Department of Youth and Community
	Development

These foundations and individuals have contributed handsomely
to Reading Reform Foundation's work over many years:
	The Annenberg Foundation
	The Leir Charitable Foundations, Inc.
	Joseph Alexander Foundation, Inc.
	The Heckscher Foundation for Children
	The Frederick P. and Sandra P. Rose Foundation
	Bloomberg
	Carnegie Corporation of New York
	Jean and Louis Dreyfus Foundation
	The Glickenhaus Foundation
	Horace W. Goldsmith Foundation
	Marc Haas Foundation
	Mary B. Horowitz
	Lucius Littauer Foundation
	The Lostand Foundation
	John J. McDonnell Margaret T. O'Brien Foundation
	Orchard Foundation
	Adam R. Rose and Peter R. McQuillan
	Deborah Rose
	The Edith Glick Shoolman Children's Foundation
	The Skirball Foundation
	TD Charitable Foundation

Also:
Louise L. Arias
Frances and Benjamin Benenson Foundation, Inc.
Corcoran Cares
Mary Ann Fribourg
Aileen Lewisohn Godsick
Faith Golding Foundation, Inc.
Mary and Michael Jaharis
The Lemberg Foundation
Nancy A. Marks
Sylvia and Leonard Marx, Jr.
Elizabeth de Picciotto
The Frank and Janina Petschek Foundation
Joanna & Daniel Rose
Diana & Jonathan F. P. Rose
Susan & Elihu Rose

Special gratitude to all the friends who attended our annual Benefit events and gave donations for 30 years, thus providing a dependable source of much-needed funds and moral encouragement.

We give profound thanks to Dr. Linnea C. Ehri and Dr. Bert Flugman of the Center for Advanced Study in Education at the Graduate School, City University of New York, for their time, effort and expertise.

Academic Partners:

The College of New Rochelle
Manhattanville College
Esther Klein Friedman

Bibliography

Adams, Marilyn Jager. *Beginning to Read: Thinking and Learning About Print.* Urbana-Champaign, Illinois: University of Illinois, 1990.

Balmuth, Miriam. *The Roots of Phonics: A Historical Introduction.* Baltimore: York Press, 1982 & 1992. Revised edition. Baltimore, Maryland: Paul H. Brookes Publishing Co., 2009.

Barzun, Jacques, *The House of Intellect.* New York: Harper and Brothers, 1959.

Chall, Jeanne S., *Learning to Read: The Great Debate.* New York: McGraw-Hill Book Company, 1967.

Chall, Jeanne S., Jacobs, Vicki A., and Baldwin, Luke E., *The Reading Crisis: Why Poor Children Fall Behind.* Cambridge, Mass.: 1990.

Flesch, Rudolf, *Why Johnny Can't Read.* New York: Harper and Brothers. 1955.

Flesch, Rudolf, *Why Johnny Still Can't Read.* New York: Harper and Brothers, 1981.

Hirsch, Jr., E.D. *The Knowledge Deficit: Closing the Shocking Education Gap for American Children.* Boston, New York: The Houghton Mifflin Co., 2006.

Orton, Samuel Torrey. *Reading, Writing and Speech Problems in Children.* New York: W. W. Norton & Company, Inc., 1937 and 1964.

Ravitch, Diane. *The Great School Wars: New York City, 1805-1973.* New York: Basic Books, Inc. 1974.

Ravitch, Diane. *The Death and Life of the Great American School System – How Testing and Choice Are Undermining Education.* New York: Basic Books, 2010.

Walcutt, Charles C., editor. *Tomorrow's Illiterates.* Boston: Little Brown & Co., 1961.

Andy Wolf wrote an initial draft on the historical background of the teaching of reading in the United States, providing some unique insights.

Studies

Anderson, Richard C., Hiebert, Elfrieda H., Scott, Judith A., and Wilkinson, Ian A.G. *Becoming a Nation of Readers: The Report of the Commission on Reading.* Washington, D.C.: The National Institute of Education, 1985.

Darling-Hammond, Linda, Wei, Ruth Chung, Andree, Alethea, Richardson, Nikole and Orphanos, Stelios. *Professional Learning in the Learning Profession: A Status Report on Teacher Development in the United States and Abroad.* The School Redesign Network at Stanford University, February, 2009.

Kober, Nancy. *Why We Still Need Public Schools: Public Education for the Common Good.* Washington, D.C.: Center on Education Policy, 2007. Founder: Jack Jennings.

National Council on Teacher Quality. *What Education Schools Aren't Teaching About Reading and What Elementary Teachers Aren't Learning.* Washington, D.C.: May 2006.

National Reading Panel. *Teaching Children to Read: An Evidence-Based Assessment of the Scientific Research Literature on Reading and Its Implications for Reading Instruction.* National Institute of Child Health and Human Development. Washington, D.C., 2000.

Exemplary Reading and Writing Programs

Bertin, Phyllis & Perlman, Eileen. *Preventing Academic Failure – A Multisensory Curriculum for Teaching Reading, Spelling and Handwriting in the Elementary Classroom.* Educators Publishing Service/School Specialty. PAFprogram.com. 2012.

Bishop, Margaret M. *The ABC's and All Their Tricks – The Complete Reference Book of Phonics and Spelling.* Milford, Michigan: Mott Media, Inc. 1986.

The Concord Review. Will Fitzhugh, Publisher.
Each year, the Review, a quarterly, selects and publishes exemplary papers in history written by secondary-school students worldwide. 730 Boston Post Road, Sudbury, Massachusetts 01776. Fitzhugh@tcr.org

Hochman, Judith C. *Teaching Basic Writing Skills – A Manual for Teachers.* Longmont, Colorado: Sopris West, 2009.

Sands, Esther Morgan, *Sands Reading Cards* (Alphabet Sound Cards, Picture Sound Cards, Letter Sound Cards). Kew Gardens, New York: Davick House, 1994. P.O. Box 150136, Kew Gardens, N.Y. 11415

Spalding, Romalda Bishop. *The Writing Road to Reading.* New York: Harper Collins Publishers, 2003.

Spector, Leona D. *Spector Phonics – A Multisensory Language Program.* New York: Leona D. Spector, 2009.

Subject-Area Reading - History

Hakim, Joy. *A History of US.* Books 1 through 10. New York: Oxford University Press, 1995.

Grades 3-8.

Subject-Area Reading – Science

Hakim, Joy. *The Story of Science – Aristotle Leads the Way.* Washington, D.C.: Smithsonian Books, 2004.

Hakim, Joy. *The Story of Science – Newton at the Center.* Washington, D.C.: Smithsonian Books, 2005.

Hakim, Joy. *The Story of Science – Einstein Adds a New Dimension.* Washington, D.C.: Smithsonian Books, 2007.

Grades 4-9.

Practical Publishing Advice

Marketing: Unmasked. Insider's Tips & Tricks for Success in Small Business Marketing, by Erik Wolf and Stephanie Frost, Atlanta, Georgia: Zudo Group, 2009.

Thank You

Recognition is hereby made of Lauren Wedeles and the many hours she devoted to editing this book. Her intrepid diligence reflects the high standards she has set for Reading Reform Foundation and herself. *Factum bene!*

Esther Morgan Sands has inspired everyone in the organization with her deep knowledge about teaching reading, combined with her warmth and good humor.

Esther's cheery greetings to everyone in each school, from the security guards to teachers, assistant principals and principals, are returned with their equal delight in seeing her. Esther's energy in the school classroom, and in giving courses to teachers, transforms students and teachers alike as she introduces them to the regularities and wonders of English.

Special mention is made of our stalwart staff:
Diane Baron
Shaketa Wheeler
Wendy Sowala

Each is contributing not only to this project but also to the continuing program in the schools.

Reading Reform Foundation stands ready to offer advice and consulting services to districts requesting it. Reading Reform Foundation can be reached at:

333 West 57th Street, Suite 1L
New York, NY 10019
Telephone: 212- 307-7320
Fax: (212) 307-0449
Email: info@readingreformny.org
Website: www.readingreformny.org

Author Biographies

Sandra Priest Rose, one of the founders of Reading Reform Foundation of New York, has worked in the New York City public schools for over fifty years, first as a volunteer, then as a teacher in the South Bronx, and finally as Chairman and Treasurer of this not-for-profit organization dedicated to training teachers in successful approaches to teaching reading, writing, spelling and comprehension. Her goal is to have every child read myths, fairy tales, history, biography, science and geography, and learn about music and art, in order to open up the world of knowledge – the rightful heritage of each child.

Glen Nelson is a freelance writer based in New York. He specializes in collaborating with business and nonprofit professionals to tell their stories in print. To date he has had three *New York Times* bestsellers. *Sunday Is for the Sun...* is his 15th book.

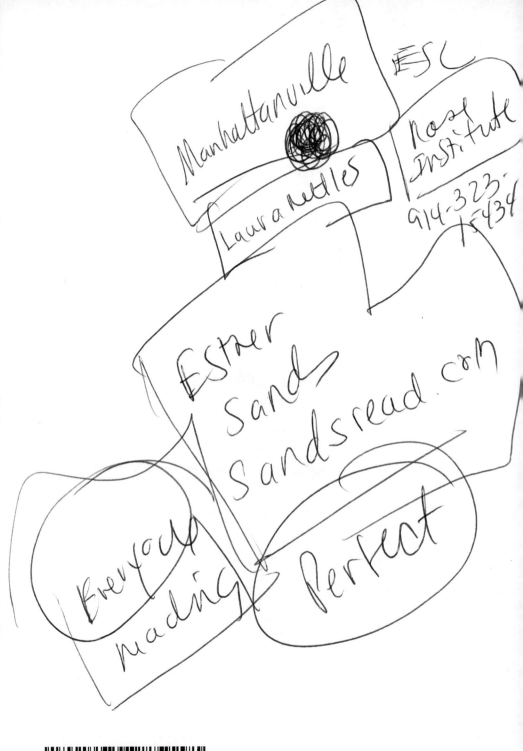

Made in the USA
Middletown, DE
18 January 2017